Taking Care

THE *CREDO* SERIES

A *credo* is a statement of belief, an assertion of deep conviction. The *Credo* series offers contemporary American writers whose work emphasizes the natural world and the human community the opportunity to discuss their essential goals, concerns, and practices. Each volume presents an individual writer's *credo,* his or her investigation of what it means to write about human experience and society in the context of the more-than-human world, as well as a biographical profile and complete bibliography of the author's published work. The *Credo* series offers some of our best writers an opportunity to speak to the fluid and subtle issues of rapidly changing technology, social structure, and environmental conditions.

Taking Care

THOUGHTS ON STORYTELLING AND BELIEF

William Kittredge

Scott Slovic, *Credo* Series Editor

Credo

MILKWEED EDITIONS

Published 1999 by Milkweed Editions
Printed in Canada
Cover design by Jeff Ess
Front-cover black-and-white photo provided by the author from his
  family album
Author photo by Geoffrey Sutton
The text of this book is set in Stone Serif.
99 00 01 02 03   5 4 3 2 1
First Edition

The author and editor wish to acknowledge Richard Hunt's and
Stacy Burton's research assistance for this project.

The epigraph on p. xvi is from Mary Oliver, "Spring," in *New and
Selected Poems* (Boston: Beacon Press, 1992), 70.

Milkweed Editions, a nonprofit publisher, gratefully acknowledges
support from our World As Home funders: Lila Wallace-Reader's
Digest Fund, and Reader's Legacy underwriter Elly Sturgis. Other
support has been provided by the Elmer L. and Eleanor J. Andersen
Foundation; James Ford Bell Foundation; Bush Foundation; Dayton
Hudson Foundation on behalf of Dayton's, Mervyn's California, and
Target Stores; Doherty, Rumble and Butler Foundation; General Mills
Foundation; Honeywell Foundation; McKnight Foundation; Minne-
sota State Arts Board through an appropriation by the Minnesota
State Legislature; Norwest Foundation on behalf of Norwest Bank
Minnesota; Lawrence and Elizabeth Ann O'Shaughnessy Charitable
Income Trust in honor of Lawrence M. O'Shaughnessy; Oswald
Family Foundation; Ritz Foundation on behalf of Mr. and Mrs. E. J.
Phelps Jr.; John and Beverly Rollwagen Fund of the Minneapolis
Foundation; St. Paul Companies, Inc.; Star Tribune Foundation; U.S.
Bancorp Piper Jaffray Foundation on behalf of U.S. Bancorp Piper
Jaffray; and generous individuals.

Library of Congress Cataloging-in-Publication Data

Kittredge, William.
    Taking care : thoughts on storytelling and belief / William
Kittredge. — 1st ed.
        p.   cm. — (Credo)
    Includes bibliographical references (p.   ).
    ISBN 1-57131-231-5 (acid-free paper). — ISBN 1-57131-232-3
(pbk. : acid-free paper)
    1. Kittredge, William—Authorship.   2. Kittredge, William—
Homes and haunts—West (U.S.)   3. Storytelling—Social aspects—
West (U.S.)   4. West (U.S.)—Civilization—20th century.   5. West
(U.S.)—Environmental conditions.   I. Title. II Series: Credo
(Minneapolis, Minn.)
PS3561.I87Z473   1999
813'.54—dc21   99-28751
    [B]   CIP

This book is printed on acid-free, recycled paper.

To Annick
Karen and Brad
Pat and Roberta
and particularly
Jo and Oscar
Richard Yates and Richard Hugo

Taking Care

Warner Valley Photo Album

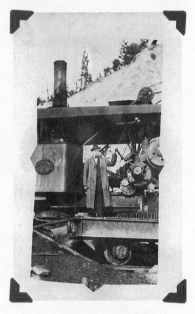

My grandfather on my mother's side, Al Meisner, a blacksmith all his life. He ran away from home in Wisconsin when he was fourteen and learned his trade in Butte, Montana, just after 1900. He was consistently the kindest adult I ever knew.

The man on the right is my grandfather, Al Meisner.

My grandparents on my father's side, William and Maude Kittredge, in front of the ranch house in Warner. At the time of this photograph, he was reputed to own the largest single acreage west of the continental divide. His mind was focused on accumulation, not elegance.

My grandfather, William Kittredge (left), and officials from the Interior Department talking over plans for Taylor Grazing Act rangeland leases in about 1945. This was at Sagehen Spring, on the highland deserts where we ran cattle in the summer.

This is my mother, Josephine, standing beside her parent's house (since demolished) on Jefferson Street in Klamath Falls, Oregon.

This is my mother, Josephine, around 1925.

My father, Oscar, in front of the cabins known ironically as "Millionaire's Row" at Odel Lake, where we always lived during the annual Fourth of July fishing trips to the cascades.

This is me pushing the boat away, my father, Oscar, standing, and his friend Henry Nicol with his back to the camera. This was taken at a reservoir in the Cascade Mountains of Oregon, during a Fourth of July fishing trip—a yearly ritual.

The MC branding crew in 1943, Ross Dollarhide on the left. (There's something of an essay about this photo in *Hole in the Sky*.)

This is the buckaroo haying crew in (I think) 1943 at the IXL Ranch my family leased from the Sheldon Wildlife Refuge on the northern Nevada border. The boy crouched on the right is me, Billy. Just out of the frame is the blacksmith shed where I branded my initials on the wall.

Me, on Lulu.

My brother, Pat, and me standing
on a woodpile at an MC branding
around 1939.

This is my cousin Sue at the IXL (1943), holding a rattlesnake she had just killed. She was fearless with snakes.

The IXL in 1943, cowhands and others on the porch (the house has long since burned). The man facing the camera is Clyde Bolton, who worked as a handyman and gardener for my father all the years I was growing up. (His wife, Ada, had much to do with my upraising.) My cousin Sue, the rattlesnake killer, is just behind Clyde.

This is my brother, Pat, on the left, me in the center, and (I think) my cousin Sue on the right, about 1939. We are trying to feed the colt, which has its head down in bucket of milk and mash. We loved it, but it died only a few days later.

This is my brother, Pat (with glasses), my sister, Roberta, and me.

How to love this world.

—Mary Oliver, "Spring"

Taking Care

Taking Care:

THOUGHTS ON STORYTELLING
AND BELIEF

by William Kittredge

At a very proper New Englandish sort of Thanksgiving dinner, at my grandmother's table, I was seated on a couple of books in a straight-backed chair beside my great Uncle Hank, a dim, lank, old alcoholic bachelor with a whiskery beard.

Uncle Hank was munching along in his silent way when he muttered some unintelligible thing and pulled his complete set of false teeth from his mouth, setting them out to dry on the fine white linen table-cloth. Hank's teeth were inextricably tangled with long strings of bright green spinach. The small child I was began whimpering. The adults, who'd been ignoring Hank, had to react. My grandmother, Hank's sister, who raised her children on a starve-to-death alkali-flat ranch, drying the rags she used for diapers on a barbed wire fence, wondered if I was always going to be such a baby. My mother, a city girl with aspirations to sing operatic arias in public, glared at her. I wish I knew if Uncle Hank was drunk that late afternoon; I wish he was here.

Uncle Hank used to lie on the lawn in front of the old white-painted ranch house where my grandparents lived when they came to visit their properties in Warner Valley, an aged man flat on his back, watching the birds as they nested. I like to think about Uncle Hank, and what he thought about as he gazed up into the poplars. He was the prime figure of failure in my family, the official eccentric, a drunk, a cautionary figure to frighten boys when they were lazy. Hank, it was said, was like a turkey. "He just pecks where he pecks." Which was as much as anybody cared to make of him in the presence of children.

I like to imagine that Uncle Hank was intimate with the habits of birds. I want to tell myself that he led a considered life, and knew it was worthwhile to spend his time utterly absorbed in the look of light through the poplar leaves.

I value Uncle Hank's indifference to the ambitions that drove my family. He refused to join their scramble to fence the world. I want to believe he was correct and not just drunk all the time. I want to think Uncle Hank loved to ride the nesting-ground swamplands in Warner, and thought grid-map plans for drainage were an abomination, a bad thing in the long run, for us and not just the muskrats and waterbirds.

If someone asked, "Who was your model of conduct when you were a child?" I might lie and say Uncle Hank. His is the great-hearted tradition in my family, or so I've come to think.

"Uncle Hank on Thanksgiving" was written in the late 1980s, as I was getting down to work on *Hole in the Sky*. It centers on themes that run through much of my writing: paradise lost, and consequent guilt. How did things go wrong? Which is of course the oldest story, interesting again only if the story in this telling is a mirror in which readers can see themselves. As I believe E. M. Forster once said, "The medium we work in is the reader's imagination."

Child in the Garden

My own story is the only one I'll ever know with any emotional accuracy. In the 1970s, when writers like Richard Yates and Richard Hugo, who believed in writing close to the bone, and in the usefulness of understanding your story, urged me to make fiction from family, I said I didn't know enough. Our family wasn't much on telling stories.

Yates told me to start small, with details. So I collected old photographs, and made lists of things like the smell of hot hydraulic oil spilled on the workshop floor when a hose was disconnected, and the worn-out look on Jake O'Rourke's face as he cleaned it up that afternoon before he died in his sleep, things that happened, year by year. I staged talks with my mother and father, and tried to itemize what I really loved, like the look of lime green poplar leaves sprung from the bud on May mornings or memories of my children fishing on Deep Creek on a summer morning, ankle deep and intent. As I lay down to sleep I tried to name the things I could never stop revering. But I could never figure out how to slide most of them into make-believe stories.

Working on *Hole in the Sky* I tried to imagine how a perfect world would look and sound and smell and feel. I tried to think people were serious when they spoke of "burning" light. Much of what follows is rewritten and recombined from attempts, at that time, to say what I thought I meant.

Owning It All was called a book of essays, *Hole in*

the Sky was called a memoir, and *Who Owns the West?* was called a meditation. They are all evidence of trying to think about what I believe, and trying to leave some residue that might be useful to others. They are texts written over texts, as this is. Ideas live in the mind, and evolve through complexities like creatures. Some multiply, interconnect, and thrive. Others fail and vanish. If you've read one or another of those books and think you're hearing it echoed here, likely you're right.

In *Hole in the Sky* I said that I wanted the luminous world to be glowing, radiant and permeable, and to be welcome in the world as I think I was when I was a child. I wanted the child who thought he was welcome to have been correct. I wanted the world to be that good. Still do.

A scab-handed wandering child who rode off on old horses named Snip and Moon, given to stoning rattlesnakes, I grew up amid the thronging presence of animals, and told of sandhill cranes at their courtship dances in our meadows. Haying and feeding and the cowherding work couldn't have been done without the help of horses.

Warner Valley, tucked against an enormous reach of Great Basin sagebrush and lava rock desert in southeastern Oregon and northern Nevada, is a hidden world. Landlocked waters flow from snowy mountains to the west but don't find a way out to the sea. They accumulate and evaporate in shallow lakes named Pelican, Crump, Hart, Stone Corral, and Bluejoint.

The late 1930s were like the last years of the

nineteenth century in Warner. What I want to get at is the isolation. We were some thirty-six gravel-road miles over the Warner Mountains from the little lumbering and rancher town of Lakeview (maybe 2,500 souls). Warner Valley was not on the route to anywhere. The way in was the way out. Sagebrush flats on the high and mostly waterless plateaus out east were traced with wagon track roads over rimrocks and saltgrass playas, waterhole to waterhole, but nobody headed in that direction with the idea of going toward the future.

Looking toward sunrise from our buckaroo camp beside the spring at South Corral, I studied the high ridge of Steens Mountain, where whores from Burns had gone to set up a summertime camp for the cowhands and sheepherders under aspen at the place called Whorehouse Meadows. Beyond lay more desert, and Idaho, the Rocky Mountains, the Mississippi, the Empire State Building, the Eiffel Tower, and pyramids in Egypt, places I had seen in books, where nobody I knew had ever gone. Or would ever go. We were not wandering people. We were located on properties.

On a mid-May morning when the homesteader's orchard back of our house was blossoming, my father was planting his garden. A hired man dumped a horse-drawn plow and a disc and a harrow out of a truck, and the next morning showed up leading a harnessed team of bay geldings. The soil was worked to perfect tilt when my father arrived with stakes and a roll of white twine, and began laying out the long precise crop rows.

We were all there in that spring light, my brother and I and my mother with my brand-new sister wrapped in blankets. My father didn't pay us much attention. This was business. He was intent on sighting down the strings, setting out six one-hundred-foot rows of strawberries (enough to keep us in crates of berries through a long run of summers), onion sets and corn in hills and peas, pole beans, squash, all in prelude to the communality of bunkhouse meals. We were spectators. Don't go running through the rows of planted spinach and chard or you will get your butt paddled. It is possible to think of that afternoon as one in a string of initiations into the values of distance and order.

An irrigation ditch wove through sandy hills from a low dam in Deep Creek canyon. Lombardy poplar rustled as I sat on my heels and studied water flowing through the little redwood weirs (called boxes) my father had built in the ditches at the head end of the garden. The water turned rainbows in the light muddied in the ditch rows and went where it had to go, soaking and seeping, inundating. Long-legged spiders walked on water. The squash blossomed, yellow jackets hummed at their business, corn grew until it was taller than I was, I stole strawberries from under the leaves, crushed stinkbugs and enjoyed their stench.

By the time I was enrolled up at the one-room Adel school, my brother and sister and cousins and I built playtime ditches and levee banks around little bare-dirt square fields we laid out with what we saw as grown-up precision beneath the apple trees outside the back door to our house. We farmed with toys, preparing for life, imitating what we knew.

In the spring of 1946 my grandfather traded off two hundred or so work teams for chicken feed. He replaced those horses with a fleet of John Deere tractors. Harnesses rotted in the barns until the barns were torn down.

My grandfather and father were irrevocably giving up on part of what they seemed to care about more than anything—their lives in conjunction to the animals they worked with. I wonder why they acted like they didn't care. Maybe they thought the world of creatures would never be denuded. I recall great workhorses running hard dry hayfields in summer before daybreak, their hooves echoing on sod as I herded them in through the mists toward the round willow-walled corral at some haycamp, and how the boy I was knew at least enough to know he loved the sound of their running, and that this was reason to revere everything in sight for another morning. If those massive horses loved this world, and they seemed to, with such satisfaction, on mornings when our breaths fogged before us, so did I.

I wish I could go to the world inside that child, reinhabit his curiosity, and know as the child knew. I want to stand out on the lawn in front of the house my father built for us and taste sour fecundity in the springtime air.

The men who worked for my father were hauling manure from the corrals on horse-drawn stoneboat sleds, rebuilding the dams across swales in the hay meadows, to flood-irrigate swamp grasses, which were turning brilliantly, variously green, sedges and field lilies and tules in the sloughs. Thickets of willow sprang to leaf. The world was accumulating an irresistible momentum.

Translucent lime green leaves emerged from the heart-shaped buds on the Lombardy poplar in front of our house and cast their tiny flitting shadows over my mother's face. Seedling oats and barley emerged in undulating drill rows across dark peat soil of swamplands broken out into plowgrounds. The lilac would soon bloom. That child had no intimation that those spring mornings would stand in memory as his approximation of perfection; his family, his life before him, the world in renewal.

Warner Valley is the main staging ground for my imagination. That boy felt like he was breathing the world into himself, and he was. His thinking is easy to remember; I recall how carefully he tried to think his thoughts through, and how he came to tell himself there was no reason for anything except for this pleasure in the love of what we are.

The waterbirds in their great vee-shaped flocks, undulating in the infinite morning sky, calling and honking, were like music we used to know, redheads, green-winged teal, and the Canadian honkers. Warner could have been the happy land, made of joyousness; maybe it was; maybe it still is.

Our ideas of the right life originate in childhood. Mine connect to that valley just as World War II was beginning. We moved to a huge new ranch, and my father built us a new house that was fresh and clean and smelled of sawdust. From a screened veranda we could see out over the wild hay meadows and willow-lined sloughs of the Thompson Field and beyond to swamplands my father was draining and farming.

Falling back into the world through a reopened gate, into a time in which we were seamlessly wedded to every thing, is a dream. I want it to be possible; I want things to be that good. But childhood is over. Our invulnerabilities are gone. Creatures, our only companions on this planet, amid the swing of infinities, are dying out. It's time to give something back to the systems of order that have supported us, some care and tenderness. We need to give some time to the arts of cherishing before much of what we adore simply vanishes. Maybe it will be like learning a skill: how to live in paradise.

Leaving the Ranch

Almost no one among the ranch people in southeastern Oregon cared about shootout Westerns. Anybody with eyes could see that they were ridiculous.

My father, I think, never voluntarily read a novel or saw a movie in his entire life. But he loved the idea of Lewis and Clark, and deeply regretted missing the opportunity to come West when the country was, as he imagined it, stone fresh and prime and new.

My mother had once aspired to sing opera, and was interested in cultural matters. Which is the reason she belonged to the Book of the Month Club, and accounts for the copy of *The Big Sky* in our house in Warner Valley. Maybe she ordered it with the thought that my father would enjoy meditating on the Mountain Man glories he missed, and spend some nights at home. But he was a man in the full power of his life, and preferred testing his genius at the poker table.

In the summer of 1948, when I was sixteen, bored and prime for enlightenment, I found the book, and fell into it. In the hayfield, I would sing Vaughn Monroe songs at top volume, and dream of wearing buckskin and walking grassy valleys along the Rockies Front. In the evening I'd go to the screened veranda, eager to fall back into connection with Boone and Teal Eye and Dick Summers. In the end I was devastated, awash in feeling.

A cautionary tale about the uses of violence, *The Big Sky* is a prelude to Cormac McCarthy's *Blood*

Meridian. Such stories constitute our *Iliad* in the West. They play off and ultimately confound our urge to imagine ourselves as dominant, thus invulnerable. Simone Weil typified such stories as "the poetry of force."

I envied the man who wrote the book, and wondered how you could come to know so much about the intricacies of life, how you could understand the plants and creatures and mountains and people as elements in a drama in which everything that happened involved every other thing that happened.

That summer I began to move toward having some politics. A. B. Guthrie Jr. helped me see where life in the American West fell into the complexities of history, and I began to sense (not something I could articulate) that we have to deal with the dark ambiguities involved in understanding what we are and why before we can hope to make sense of our purposes, or believe in our own usefulness.

By the 1950s I was in college, avoiding the war in Korea and aimlessly majoring in agriculture. In the winter of my sophomore year at Oregon State, studying technological farming, drifting through classes in agronomy and soil science, close to flunking out of college, it came to me as I tried to fathom the intricacies of intermediate algebra that I was, probably incurably, useless.

The young women we knew, boys like me, seemed to inhabit another country, where they laughed and lived by rules that were incomprehensible. Boys like me thronged in the jock fraternities, running in packs and yearning for unlikely athletic careers, erecting great walls of boisterousness. For weeks after recognizing my uselessness I lived in intimacy with no one but my new companion, my ceaseless regret that I was, irrevocably it seemed, what I was.

Then it snowed, a rare thing in the lowlands of the Willamette Valley, great slow flakes in the gray feathery light. By nightfall we were snowballing and eventually ambushed from behind a wall of snowy lilac by hilarious women.

A snowball broke my glasses, cut my nose, and brought her to me. She was dark-eyed and strong, utterly what I took to be gorgeous. "Lord," she said, "look at you." She folded my broken glasses into her pocket. "Come on," she said. How could this be? Her name, she said, when I didn't ask, was Janet. "What's yours?" she asked. As she waited I began to understand that despite my incapacities another life was possible.

Deep in that same night, when Janet had gone home to the Chi Omega house and I was in my fraternity, upstairs on the cold sleeping porch, my friends and I were awakened by news of a terrible accident. Two men I admired, captains of the football team, one a former roommate of mine, had been riding sleds towed along the icy streets at reckless speed behind an automobile. At an intersection they had swung into the path of an oncoming pickup truck, and had been crushed, killed.

Curled tight under my old Hudson Bay blanket, a

gift from my father, shaking, trying to imagine what would happen now, I at least understood that I didn't know how to grieve for anyone but myself, and I thought something like *she'll forgive me, when I tell her.* These decades later, our children grown, living a far distance from one another, it is impossible to know what she saw in me, or wanted, or what I could have felt beyond a boyish drive to ease my isolation, but I have to think the last thing Janet was looking for that snowy night was someone to forgive.

Nineteen, and married, an intense young man seeking models, in love, planning for eternity (Janet and I were married in an Episcopalian ceremony), I was trying to figure out who I was, and deeply frightened by the process. Without facing it, I think now, I was already trying to avoid going back to the ranch to live among people who understood devotion to work and accumulation as the principle attributes of a useful man. I was becoming the wrong boy in the wrong place.

In an American literature class I came upon Emerson, Thoreau, and Whitman, Melville and Hemingway, and Faulkner's bear in the wilderness. Finally, words that mattered, and resonated in the mind of a boy who learned his values in the presence of waterbirds and horsemen. Reasons to attempt thinking. I fell for books, and ideas. Emerson said, "Nothing is at last sacred but the integrity of your own mind."

Nothing else, in that first ego-driven exposure

to the possibility of thinking, was even interesting. But the news that Thoreau and Whitman began rural was reassuring; they'd made lives as writers. Maybe I wasn't useless, or even crazy. Maybe I could be like them.

In 1953 I sat over Hemingway on winter afternoons in the Willamette Valley, gazing out to incessant rain, recalling a hot quiet twilight and the exact feel of casting to specific holes in little high desert creeks—I could see the precise look of dark boulders, water cutting and folding back and the trout flashing, and I was able to care for myself and how I had grown up, and sorrow for my losses. "Big Two-Hearted River" moved me to forget the reading. Light fell through the willow leaves, and I saw reflections on the surface of water and lights refracted in the moving depths.

Afternoons spent watching into fishing water resonated with significances, electric trout in the swirl. Hemingway was reassuring. The trickiness Nick Adams endured during the sad processes of initiation into an American manhood was something I surely knew about. Everything beyond afternoons on the fishing stream, as Scott Fitzgerald said about football, was slightly anticlimactic. I was sure of that as I watched rain misting into the Willamette Valley. But I was young and I knew I didn't know much. I would outgrow common despair, I knew I would.

Reading Hemingway, I was awash with admiration, and thought maybe I could live a life of consequence if I could write with his ringing accuracy. So

I took a short story writing class taught by Bernard Malamud, who wanted us to write stories that turned on recognitions, moments of enlightenment (the same thing I wanted from my own students for decades): I thought the notion was utterly false.

What interested me were anecdotal celebrations. What I saw in my mind's eye as I thought about stories was rain in the summer and men braiding ropes in the hayloft of the barn at the Coleman Ranch in Nevada, where the buckaroo outfit from Warner sometimes camped. At night in the cookhouse, to the flickering light of a lantern, they told about killer dogs named Donner und Blitzen, from the country over east around Steens Mountain, whose spirits prowled the darkness. Knowing it was foolish but spooked anyway, I ran through the darkness to the barn, where my bedroll was spread on a mattress of hay. Back in the cookhouse, I knew, those men were laughing, shaking their heads, and changing the subject to descriptions of women.

What I should be trying to write, I thought, were stories about those men doing what they always did, and Steens Mountain on the horizon in its timelessness. But Malamud said stories were about change. I wasn't interested. What I wanted to write about were moments when nothing changed.

For me there was no significant world but Warner. The horsemen I knew were the real people; their knowledge was real knowledge (the rest was town stuff, and unreal; it didn't count). I wrote about an old cowhand who went down to the butchering with a white ceramic cup he filled with blood when a jugular was cut, and how he drank from it with great smiling relish. We thought maybe he loved the taste of blood; we thought maybe he was crazy. But that's as far as my story went. Nobody, including me at the time of that writing, the college boy in Corvallis, suspected that ranchhand with his white ceramic cup had any politics. We never imagined (or so I like to believe; who knows what my father imagined?) that he might be crazy with the anger of the outcast, the disenfranchised, that maybe he was showing his willingness to face into the bloodiness without flinching, without any prettying up. Which is what I tend to think now.

Many people in the outback West felt and still feel they have been left behind by a world culture traveling toward some unknown destination at warp speed; they feel betrayed, and some are furious. But I didn't understand. My politics at that time were anchored to nostalgia; I wrote vignettes. Malamud flunked them, one after another. I wanted the old world of my childhood; I wanted it to hold still; I didn't want to think about reasons for change. I wrote up mornings when we (boys) were sent out alone to drive the herd of buckaroo saddle horses across the sagebrush distances to some new camp on an old wagon track road, our sense of importance in the silence as those horses drifted over the white alkaline playas. I was trying to recreate dreams. Malamud never did get me to understand the ways stories worked, how they were primarily useful when they helped us see freshly. I came away convinced that success as a writer depended on inauthenticity. This is a cautionary tale. It is centered on looking back, to see where you went wrong in another life. But, for me, it's also a celebration of the kind I wanted to write when I started. I'd learned, in that cowhand existence, that quitting was the unforgivable thing. I kept attempting to write, thinking of myself as someone who *would* write even when I'd quit trying.

After four pointless years in the Air Force, in the fall of 1958, Janet and I went home to the ranch. (Again, this is material from *Owning It All,* reworked in *Hole in the Sky,* and another time here.) I lacked the imagination to think up another future. Time-serving had deeply eroded my will to see myself as other than affectless and bored.

In Warner, waterbirds were still flying north to the tundra, and my family was deep into agribusiness. In 1936, deep in the Great Depression, when my grandfather bought the MC Ranch with no down payment, the valley was mostly swamps. My father bought his first track-layer, an RD6 Caterpillar he used to start building a seventeen-mile diversion canal designed to carry spring run-off east of the valley. He was on the way to draining the entire valley. He bought another Caterpillar, an RD7, and a John Deere combine that cut an eighteen-foot swath, then two D7s; the diversion canal was finished by 1940; the natural drainages were squared into a network of dragline ditches. Shallow lakes were pumped dry; peat beds left by ancient decaying swampland remnants were diked into undulating grainfields—Houston Swamp with 750 acres, Dodson Lake with 800—vast fields, which were flooded, pumped dry, and farmed—a total of 8,000 acres. My family was falling deep into a dream about power.

The irrigation system was a masterpiece of complexity. We could run the water around and around on a dry year, pumping it back to the high ground, to reuse—until it wore out was the joke. My father built beautiful redwood headgates and named the junctions where our canals ran together Four Corners and Center Bridge. We acted like naming made the valley entirely ours. My father bought three more John Deere combines, and settled in to a cycle of farming— flooding the fields, draining and tillage, seeding, harvesting—that continued for two decades.

Then, in April of 1959, a few months after I got back from the Air Force, my grandfather fell insensible from his chair at a table with other pinochle players. He would not regain consciousness.

Soon, although I didn't know what I was doing, I was in charge of our farming in Warner Valley, raising alfalfa hay and barley to support an industrial feedlot. Grown to be a man, I had inherited the work my father left when he moved on in a run of family trouble. Despite the mud and endless hours, that work remained play for years, making things both functional and elegant, craftsmanlike work, artistic and practical, creating order according to an ideal based on efficiency.

The most intricate part was called "balancing water," a night and day job involving headgate valves and redwood weirs and eighteen-inch drainage pumps. I learned to understand flowing water in Warner as a surgeon understands the flow of blood across a chart of human anatomy. Irrigation was one of the prime playthings in my life (the finest, next to writing). You can lose decades in such work. People do. For years, I loved it. What a pleasure it was, work that was like art.

Crouching in imitation of men I'd watched in childhood and movies, I crumbled warm friable peat between my fingers. It smelled of acrid rot and swampiness, bacterial life. My regard for that odor, which came of working light and air into soil, a stink we earned, was an utter surprise, a discovery of purpose. I thought I'd found the most valuable thing, work to absolve and absorb my life. Farming was a constuctive thing to do, a stay against pointlessness and a reason for giving myself away.

Preoccupied with ditches and headgates, flowing water, I thought this was spiritual work, and useful, participating in glories, seeds in moist soil springing green shoots up into the light, to be food. The seasonal run of irrigating and farming and threshing would always be worth doing.

Trying to write about that farming eventually got me started thinking about the possibility that a habitable paradise on earth could be constructed, as in gardens. I imagine Warner Valley as a vast blossoming garden, thronging with gardeners and surrounded, as it was in my childhood, by what at least seemed to be wildness, vast tracts where native ecologies would still turn through their infinitely complex transactions, where biodiversity could survive. As our old Hemingway said, "Isn't it pretty to think so."

For what we regarded as commonsense reasons our work became increasingly industrialized. We reinvented the water flow patterns in the valley using a model copied from industry, and in the process had irrevocably altered the ecology of our lives, moving into the system of monied technology that is agribusiness.

We worked all through the daylight and the night, in a twenty-four-hour-a-day frenzy that began around April 25 and ended—with luck—by the tenth of May, just as leaves on the Lombardy poplar were breaking their buds, two hundred acres in a shift, three thousand acres in twenty days with our four D7 Caterpillars, track-layers we called them, and the old RD6, working the ground in what we thought of at the time as a sort of conquest of acreage. The rumbling and clatter of diesel engines was the sound of pure energy. Everyone was willing to sacrifice in order to get the work done. The work was like war, exciting and a consuming purpose, and I loved it while I thought we were winning.

In late June we started cutting alfalfa with a half-dozen swathers. We baled with three-wire balers. The barley was harvested in August and September, and the aftermath was burned—along with more combustible peat soil. We sprayed fields with 2-4-D ethyl and malathion and the German World War II nerve gas called parathion (for clover mites in barley), and we shortened our own lives. We baited coyotes with 1080, hunted them from aircraft, and as a consequence rodent populations exploded and destroyed our alfalfa. Our peat soils began to go saline. We couldn't hire anybody who cared enough about our mechanical work to do it right. Men who hired out as ranchhands in the 1960s were missing the boat and knew it. They despised the work, and themselves for doing it.

On a hill above the old buckaroo camp we built an industrial mill to process feed for endless lots of fattening cattle, chopping alfalfa hay, rolling barley, adding molasses and growth-inducing chemicals like silbesterol, a howling, stinking place where work proceeded at a pace determined by machines, an arm of our intentions gone mechanical. We cleaned manure from the vast sequence of feed lots with D7 Cats and scrapers. Our dreams had led us to these processes.

Calculating to insure that our work was efficient and thus profitable, we distanced ourselves from caring for one another and aspects of the world most of us loved in our secret hearts, like peat-bog swamps where the muskrats swam and the waterbirds nested, and black lava rock rims to the east, and the silence of autumn under the white sky. We worked at strip-mining a fertile property in order, we thought, to do God's work, and raise food, create order. We thought such work justified almost anything. We were living a yeoman's dream, constructing a good cultivated place, an invaluable effort in our myth of the right life, although nobody would talk about work that way.

We reinvented our properties in accordance with the most pervasive ideal provided by our culture. We had perfected a mechanical way of proceeding, and had reshaped our world according to the dictates of a mythology that revered efficiency. The reward was enormous power over what is called "nature," while we used people and our homeland as things.

The beloved waterbirds no longer came to Warner in great migratory flights. We had drained and plowed their marshy habitat. Our fields were increasingly lifeless. Bacterial life in the soils was poisoned by our chemicals and dying. We thought we were living the right lives. But our mythology had told us a simple-minded lie. The world would not stop evolving.

In 1964, reading *Silent Spring*, I discovered that I was inhabiting an absolute double bind. We were wrecking what we did not leave untouched. I felt enormously betrayed. I loved my work but learned to hate its consequences. The essence of what we were doing, as I came to think of it, can quickly be understood during a visit to a meatpacking plant. Our product was feed, and fattened animals, for slaughter. Watch the animals as they are killed and cut up. The odor of blood hangs in the air like mist. I couldn't see the oftentimes glorious and solacing intracacies of actual life. My days were semi-unendurable.

There was an afternoon on a ditchbank with a dented bucket of orange carrot slices marinated in strychnine, poisoning badgers, when I dreaded every moment I could forsee. All things seemed equally unreal, my hand in the rubber glove, holding the slice of carrot, which was almost luminous, clouds over Bidwell Mountain, the sound of my breathing. I would have to move soon if I was ever going to get home. I was numb with dread, sorrowing for myself because I felt nothing but terror. This had to be craziness. There is no metaphor for that condition; it is precisely like nothing.

We never learned to speak of the fact that the place where we practiced our husbandry was of more than economic value. We farmed in naive and heartless ways, insisting that we could reap and not repay the flowering world without eventual consequence.

Eventually I had to enter some rooms in which old working men were dead; I had to see to their burying, and notice they were not grieved for by much of anybody but me; I had to acknowledge the degree to which they had been used and abandoned. In springtime I had to admit that the waterbirds were not going north in huge flocks anymore. Peat soils were going saline and blowing away. I had to admit that my work was one of the reasons these things were happening. I had to embrace my responsibility for the wearing out, men dying in the bunkhouse.

But I couldn't imagine doing my work according to any other model. Born to the ruling class, it was my responsibility to make the world go; I had no other work. I was fated, so I thought, to participate in the diminishment of things I cherished, and that idea made me crazy.

The rules of the agricultural society I had grown up in looked inviolable. I was not strong-minded enough to reimagine them, so I transformed myself into an intellectual who didn't feel responsible for anything beyond sympathy. I read my books. It would be my job, as a man who wished to be a writer, to be a witness. But I had no point of view toward the things I'd seen, no intentions. I was lost.

In the late autumn when the vast flocks of waterbirds were flying south through our valley in Oregon, I would take my old Remington shotgun and go out to kill in the afternoons. For a while when I was in my early thirties, I was diverted from my sense of pointlessness.

On good days, I loved the flare of birds against a bright morning and the flash of flame from shotguns fired into the twilight sky. But, trying to imitate the ardor I'd seen in my father and the men he hunted with, I soon began to sense the degree to which I was fraudulent and attempting to trick myself.

There's the old business, killing to eat, and there's *enactment,* killing for sport, both ritual and game, but never necessary. I began to feel like hunting was a playground sport, alienating rather than sustaining, a game of conquest involving death. I took to fishing on Deep Creek, rediscovering remnants of my mind while studying the wash of creekwater around volcanic rocks and trying to drift a red and white Renegade just into the attention of some nervous trout. For a while I relocated myself inside rituals of knot tying and fly casting. Then I stopped fishing and just watched the fish at their feeding, the hatch of insects in the slanting twilight. It sort of cured what I took to be my craziness. I learned to value trout because I could participate in their freedoms by being nearby.

By the time I was thirty-four, I'd given up on blood sports and spent my autumns looking forward to the downhill ski season. It was easier on the soul. By that time my father had himself given up hunting. He spent his last years watching the fog banks and waves come in over a cold rocky seacoast from the Pacific.

Convinced that ranching was meaningless, I was frantic with anxiety, unable to catch my breath or think I could think. In order to save myself, I started trying to write. Over weeks and months what had been a slowly accumulating intention began to become resolve. On the day after Thanksgiving in 1964, hungover and thirty-two years old, I sat down and told myself that I would write each day, giving it a lifetime of effort whether it worked or not. Success wasn't the point. I'd get up early and type a while before going off to the grain camp and breakfast. Here's the first page of that first story (all that I saved). It was called "Sorrow In L.A. County":

> The day after the day after the day after. Jerry Benidict was a thin and handsome young man, married seven years to the same girl and in his secret heart an altogether special person.

Nothing seemed to register for the first long seconds except that today was the day after something.

His head was going to burst like a pain bomb. (Long seconds at first seemed to register nothing except anxiety about who he was and what). Then he rolled over on the bed and knew something had happened to the Jerry Benidict who lived in a division house in the Thousand Oaks district. A house that shown like pink spangled coral in the great yellow California sun, that same sun that was slanting into his eyes through the dirty venetian blinds in this furnace of a dingy, crappy, cheap noon-time motel room.

Great Jesus suffering Christ where in hell was this? And why in thundering throbbing hell was he here?

Rolling his feet out on the warping linoleum floor Jerry the boy hung his head and knew only one thing, that he was familiarly and wonderfully hungover and that this little room was an airtight oven that he had to get out of because it was the day after the day after Patty the girl bride in the little pink bungalow had lumped his clothes in his suitcases for the third time in the last four years and dismissed him from the presence of herself and her two little girl babies.

He was hungover, really tightened up, and he resented it all because there . . .

There, mercifully, the page ends.

I didn't understand what I was attempting. I thought it was making sentences and paragraphs, fashioning elegance. I saw no dynamic working in the world except for the one in which people were ruined by time, which I took to be the master story of all creation. I thought it summed things up. I didn't know my job was mainly trying to see through to coherencies, and that the seeing would have to be done over and over since we are always partway wrong.

Late in 1967 we sold the ranch in Warner. My father and my mother had been divorced for more than a decade. My own family broke apart (Janet and the children went off to another life in California). At that moment of great difficulty, when I was living alone in a cabin on the Klamath Marsh, on a bright cold morning, snow two feet deep and windows opaque with frost, my father and I made contact. My father sipped a glass of Jack Daniels, and asked me what I was going to do with myself. (This is an anecdote I rework and rework, an example of the release that can come when someone tells you a story that lights up what you know from a fresh perspective.)

When I told him I was going back to college, with the idea of trying to learn how to be a writer, I halfway expected him to shake his head and laugh. Runaway career moves were not considered remotely appropriate for ranchmen. What I was telling him— that trying to write seemed like my one chance to turn into someone I wanted to be—even in my mind reeked of secret agendas, failure, and panic, my need to escape.

What I wasn't telling him, which he must have known anyway, was the degree to which I didn't want to be like him, and didn't want to give my life to an enterprise I didn't value. But those weren't lines of thought I could articulate. I was willing to pretend I was a fool confessing to weakness. I would have been happy in that role. But my father didn't give me a chance. "Do what you want," he said. "I've done things I hated all my life. I sure as hell wouldn't recommend that."

My idea of myself, who I was, and should be, rolled over. My father—through an act of the imagination—gave me the permission I needed, to be whatever I could manage.

In the end, maybe always, he believed we are sustained by our willingness to chance the results of freedom. From that time on we were friends. Although it was not a thing we talked about, we understood ourselves as subversives together. He gave me courage to leave the life I had grown up in, and head out for other shores. Running before the winds of emotion, I was gone. My father's advice, as I see it now, was utterly political.

Learning to Think

In 1969, at age thirty-six, I got a degree in creative writing from the University of Iowa and lucked into a teaching job at the University of Montana (there weren't many other places I would have survived in academia). Missoula was thick with writers like Dick Hugo and Dorothy Johnson and Jim Welch and Jim Crumley, and their friendship and advice sustained me for decades, not that we spent a lot of time talking about the actual processes of getting words on the page. They seemed happy to see me become whatever I could manage. I was still frantic but I knew Missoula was home.

In 1976, Crumley and Steve Krauzer and my brother Pat and I traveled to Sun Valley, Idaho, with the idea of hanging out at a conference on Western film. Looking for a playpen, I encountered Western intellectuals for the first time. I began thinking about purposes and politics, and what it meant to be a citizen of the American West.

Which was a good thing, since I was as far adrift as ever. I'd gone back to writing with the intention of celebrating people and places I loved. But by 1976 that intention was running dry. I'd published a number of short stories, and felt like I'd said what I had to say. Nostalgic stories were already seeming repetitive and self-imitative (it was probably a mistaken way to think—artists often spend their careers working specific emotional terrain, witness Faulkner and Virginia Woolf, and my friends Dick Hugo and Ray Carver).

But I wanted to claim new territory, and couldn't find any. And it wasn't likely I'd be able to find an entirely satisfying life in nothing but teaching. Richard Yates, when I first started looking for a university job, said, "You're a writer, not a teacher. Keep your priorities in order. Teaching comes second." Teaching was "something to do in the afternoon." Yates was horrified by the prospect of uttering halfway nonsensical abstractions and watching students copy them down. He was talking about the possibility of coming to believe in your own bullshit, learning to pontificate as a way of going dead, killing any possibility of being a true witness.

So, the summer of 1976, at that Western film conference in Sun Valley, I was afloat, without definable purposes, and ripe to find new ones. And there they were, before me. The West, it turned out, was actually interesting, an intellectual topic. At lectures by people like Richard Slotkin, I took notes, and began trying to think about mythologies and politics. The next summer, in Missoula, Steve Krauzer and I taught a course on the Western, seventeen movies on seventeen afternoons, some of which we'd not seen before the class. We cowrote nine formula Western novels, the Cord Series. All that work, for me, was a start toward rethinking my own purposes. It was the beginning of an education in political implications, one more way of leaving the ranch.

Through the late 1970s and early 1980s I went on attending conferences at Sun Valley. They were stage-managed by Richard Hart, who was a genius at bringing a spectrum of thinkers together before a topic like "Inventing the West," hoping they'd be excited into a run of speculation and thinking on their feet. I found my semi-educated self giving a talk with the preeminent Western historians William Goetzmann and Alvin Josephy there in the front row. My attention was vividly focused that terrifying morning. I asked my brainless questions, and I listened to the patient answers. As the West goes on rethinking itself, a lot of the impetus comes from people who got to know one another during the years at Sun Valley. Hard questions were asked; surprising answers resulted. Conferences most often center on old friends knitting some network of privileges back together. But those put on by Richard Hart went immediately beyond that, and were for me invaluable.

In 1977 (much of this is from the latter pages of *Hole in the Sky*) I began what I profoundly hope is a lifelong romance with Annick Smith, who has been the luck of my life, a widow of Hungarian/Jewish ancestory, mother of four grown men, and willing to stay humane no matter how disconcerted she may be in her heart, or pissed off at the wayward fragility of things. She is a good deal less flighty than I when ultimate chips are falling. While their children watched, she spent half an hour crouched and trying to force breath back into her husband's mouth after he had fallen into death on their kitchen floor. Annick has been tempered by circumstances in ways that I have not.

Annick and I toured my home country a year later, a ritual of courting that makes sense to me. North from Reno, past Pyramid Lake and towns like Gerlach and Vya, we came into the rangelands where my family had run cattle. In sunset light we were stunned by what looked to be an infinity of antelope in grazing bands of two or eight or fifteen on the grassy edges of an alkaline playa. They paid us none of their sweet attention, but went on grazing in intricate syncopation, leaving us lost in a sight from the enormous isolations of the past. I eased her four-wheel-drive Subaru down a lava rock road the MC buckaroo cook had traveled with a four-horse chuck wagon, over the rimrock into Guano Valley. The old L-shaped ranchhouse under cottonwoods, where cowhands slept in canvas bedrolls spread on splintery floors, had burned. In the blacksmith shop where they heated horseshoes and shaped them on the anvil to fit the hooves of desert-traveling horses, I was jolted by my initials—BK—branded on the wall.

The thirteen-year-old boy, bored on a Sunday, had cranked up the forge and heated an iron rod red hot and carefully burned his initials into a plank wall in that little building, trying to name his connection to the doings of the men he was learning to work with.

I felt blessed when Annick discovered flowers in the rimrocks above Sage Hen Springs. As a boy I'd never noticed flowers. She was comfortable with silences ringing over the distances. We stood at ten thousand feet, at daybreak on the ridgetop that is

Steens Mountain, with a great rockfall to the alkaline playa of the Alvord Desert at our backs. Mount Adams, far away in Washington, hung snowy and dim on the horizon like a phantom sail. The air was alive with a wash of ozone left from lightning storms. We were gazing out to country I see in the eye of my mind when trying to tell myself who I am: out across Catlow Valley, where the homesteaders lured West by railroad promotions built their cabins and failed in such absolute ways in the 1920s, and West Road Gulch in the Beatty Buttes where we made a sport of killing dozens of rattlesnakes one morning when I was a boy, and the Hart Mountain escarpment (which I only see as I saw it from the fields of Warner, luminous in the light of the 1960s).

The shallow lakes in North Warner were brimming with spring run-off, shimmering in the morning, edged with green and populated by rafts of white pelicans and snow geese, like a dream of what the world could be if we let it, alive and significant without us. With Annick I began trying to shut down my incessant self-preoccupied puzzling, and experience what is. I felt like the lost piece falling into a puzzle.

In 1978 Annick and her partner Beth Ferris were deep into the processes of trying to shape and produce a feature film about the life of a woman named Eleanor Stewart, who had gone to backland Wyoming in 1911, and written a book about her time there, which is in print to this day. It is called *Letters of a Woman*

Homesteader. That fall I was invited to rework Beth's script, not because I knew anything about scripts but with the idea that my ranch background might contribute authenticity. I knew about things like harnesses and skinning dead animals. But I thought I knew more. I wrote lots of new dramatic scenes and pouted when the director, Richard Pearce, a consummate professional, didn't think they were so hot.

But, occasionally, I had the wit to pay attention to what was actually going on. Early in 1979, as the film was being shot at an abandoned homestead near the Snowy Mountains out in the center of Montana, Richard Pearce asked me to reimagine a scene. I went up in the old Graves Hotel in Harlowtown, and got down to work. But my new scene didn't excite anybody. I wrote another, and another. When I came down with the seventh, each different except for the emotional transaction at the core, I found that the second one was going to be shot the next day. It played, and was clearly the best thing I contributed to *Heartland.* I still take pride in watching it.

That day taught me a lesson about discipline and insisting that the work be done as perfectly as possible. (A lot, of course, depends on how "perfect" is defined—vast seas of sloppiness have been excused by people like me claiming the right to perfect self-expression.)

During those same weeks I was also getting an education in the arts of the personal essay. I'd gotten a call from Terry McDonnel, an editor of *Outside* magazine I'd met in San Francisco over Thanksgiving.

He wanted me to write an essay for the first issue of a glossy new publication he was starting, called *Rocky Mountain Magazine*. "Can't do it," I said. "Don't know how."

"I'll tell you," Terry said, and he did, on the phone, in a few minutes. What he wanted was a series of scenes in what constituted an emotional progression, witnessed by a figure (the author) who is trying to fathom their meaning. Sort of like a detective story, he said, a learning and teaching story leading to a recognition and implication of the consequences, for both witness, maybe those involved in the acting out, and certainly the reader (this is my language). Terry asked for some ideas. I laboriously worked out a couple and sent them, along with a couple of titles with no ideas attached. One of the titles was "Redneck Secrets." Which he liked.

So I found myself trying to figure out just what secrets rednecks might be harboring, and at last saw that this was a chance to write about actual moments and people (material I'd never been able to work into the motion of a story). I found I loved writing about things that had really happened. Terry gave me permission to speak my mind about significances (briefly, he said I could have 10 percent of the essay for what he called "your bullshit"). It was like getting out of jail.

For years my essay writing classes at the University of Montana built on what I'd learned from Terry McDonnel, focusing on work that began with experience and then attempted to transcend the personal, writing that began with a voice capable of talking and speculating in candid, trustworthy ways. It then moved to defining significant experiences, to finding patterns, and gesturing toward social implications. But how to define trustworthy?

Writers, I think, should try to make clear, as a way of attempting honesty, tricks that are working in their storytelling. Bringing up the idea of social implications (as in this instance), is a way of implicitly promising the reader that the text will eventually come to closure around those ideas, thus "hooking" them (we talked a lot about the legitimacy of "implied promises"). But our lives turn on working within processes, and not on imposing closure. Exploration and rethinking were the point of things. The work should go to the reader as a gift, to be used.

But maybe such thinking is just a way of trying to legitimize my own writing, much of which is made of fragmentary explorations, told and retold in an attempt to get closer to what I mean to say (occasionally these were sorted into a book). This text is a continuation of that process, work reassembled and often rewritten, along with some new writing, as I kept trying to think during the autumn of 1998.

Rediscovering Home

Westerners tend to think of themselves as a society of mostly decent people who are lucky enough to live in connection to wildness (much of this comes from a variety of magazine essays that were written after *Hole in the Sky,* and incorporated into *Who Owns the West?*). Westerners most often despise people who lust for power and property. The West exists in our national imagination as an enclave where people can find the flowering abundance that they imagine as having once-upon-a-time existed everywhere in the New World, where they can live in good-hearted, generous proximity to their native inclinations. Families find communities in which to farm, vote, tend the hardware store, raise children, hunt elk every fall, and pray to God in any manner they like. Self-realization (not conventional success) is considered the prime virtue.

On spring days in Montana, as you approach St. Ignatius on the Flathead Indian Reservation, you can find yourself stunned by the glittering alpine peaks in the Mission Mountains, glaciers against a perfect bluebird sky. In the valley along Post Creek the willows are opening new leaves, and the hayfields are greening up.

The little city where I live, Missoula, lies at the conjunction where the Big Blackfoot River and the Bitterroot River join the Clark's Fork of the Columbia. Rattlesnake Creek, which flows through town, originates in a Wilderness Area just outside the city limits.

So much water (to echo Carver), such fly-fishing, so close to home.

In 1805 one of our first wayfarers in the West, Meriwether Lewis, sat beguiled beside the thunderous falls of the Missouri River (since dammed for hydroelectric power) and told himself this West was not only the great useful place Jefferson had instructed him to discover, treasure for the republic, but also sublime, by which he likely meant it reeked of obscurity, privation, vacuity, solitude, silence, boundlessness, and, thus, of almost infinite possibility. As it still sort of does.

Montana reaches six hundred miles from remnants of maritime cedar tree forests near the Idaho border to the meeting of the Missouri River and the Yellowstone near the North Dakota border, and splits into two kingdoms, divided along the Front Range of the Rockies. In western Montana the water flows to the Columbia and the Pacific; in eastern Montana it flows to the Missouri and the Mississippi and the Gulf. If state lines in the West had been laid out in the natural and sensible way explorer and geographer John Wesley Powell called for a hundred years ago, along watershed lines, Montana would be two states, each more coherent.

Western Montana, where I live, is a land of alpine mountains and farmland valleys, Yellowstone and Glacier National Parks, and great wilderness areas. In the Beartooth-Absoroka Wilderness along the northern edge of Yellowstone Park people hike for days above ten thousand feet in elevation, on trails through blue and yellow fields of delicate wildflowers. The waters of glacial tarns mirror snowfields on stony peaks. In autumn you can horse-pack into the Bob Marshall Wilderness along the Rockies Front, and photograph rutting, bugling elk in meadows beside the Sun River. It's claimed there are more elk in that country than there were when Lewis and Clark came by, and that the Rockies Front is the largest recovering big game range in the world.

We talk about those animals as "game" in wilderness we go to in order that we might renew intimacy with a version of the place where we evolved in company with other animals, our only companions in the vast universe. Isolate humans too long and we start getting nervous, crazy, unmoored, inhabited by diseases we cannot name, driven to thoughtless ambitions and easy cruelties. We see it everywhere, in the newspaper, so many, so isolated, gone so frantic.

Contact with the evolving world is experience that comes to us like a gift in Montana; we look up and find ourselves in intimacy with things as they have always been in the history of our species, contact that to me is sacred, by which I mean necessary, and a reason many of us stay forever.

In eastern Montana the short-grass plains roll across enormous distances of seemingly infinite variety. I go out into the beauty of frozen winter landscapes between towns like Jordan and Circle and rivers like the Musselshell and the Tongue, hear the silence ringing, and sense that the thronging world is not so overcrowded by civilizations after all. I stand by a fence line in the shimmering of summer heat over white houses and red barns isolated amid the yellow wheatland and fallow plow ground strips alternating across the country northeast of Great Falls, and romance myself with the idea that it's a place where I could settle into dreams while the world went on without my troubles.

Most Westerners live in the cities, like Denver and Phoenix, but the West I revere is made up of small settlements, many rough-edged and isolated, held together by hard-handed self-respect, and not much money. On the road in Montana, I have a drink and talk with the locals in country taverns like the Jersey Lily in Ingomar, on the plains north of the Yellowstone River. People there tend to be mostly open-minded and irreverent if condescending toward a man so foolish as to live full-time in town. "But you got to get around, all the same," a man told me. "I go to Seattle. I could eat them oysters three meals a day." He stared toward the far-off horizon, and I wondered if he was seeing a platter stacked with shaved ice, and a dozen freshly cracked Belons on the half-shell. And another dozen.

The West is a place where independence and minding your own business are regarded as prime virtues. Many people who come want to escape the cramping and compromises involved in living in, as one very successful escapee put it, "the more thickly populated dens of society." Some seek a new life.

Others were driven. The Sioux and Cheyenne

and Blackfeet and Crow drifted to the plains after the pressure of white settlement forced them from their homelands in the forests north and west of the Great Lakes. Fur trappers and the buffalo hunters followed, and the U.S. military. After hideous genocidal warfare (it's claimed, and believed, that white traders deliberately gave the Blackfeet smallpox with a gift of infected blankets), the Indians were confined to reservations, making way for the gold camp miners and cattlemen from Texas and railroaders from Chicago and wave after wave of homesteaders. Some stayed, and made a killing. Others starved out. Some stayed anyway, however tough it got.

The West was a place where good people could come to escape the injustices of an old world. Valleys between shining mountains, and wetland enclaves out in vast sagebrush and lava rock distances—they were refuge for enormous migrations of the oppressed from Europe and (despite racism) from Asia. The West was where opportunity lived, and freedom, if you were tough enough.

But the West was also an extraction colony, to be worked, where the strong could grow rich. Fur trappers, miners, ranchers, and loggers came wave after wave, intent on making a killing. They dug holes in the earth, cut the ancient trees for lumber with which to build towns, killed off the wild animals so they could replace them with grazing herds, plowed up prairies, dammed rivers, and got busy pumping the aquifers dry.

Such adventurers were often ruthless, heroes in

the mythology of the Western, a legend of conquest designed to reveal violence—poisoning the badger, strapping on guns, building the great dam—as a way of ultimately solving problems.

A hundred and fifty years ago some sixty million buffalo roamed the North American prairies. The last wild ones, at least in the stories I've heard, were shot south of Jordan in 1886, by William Hornaday, for the Smithsonian; he returned to Washington, D.C., with twenty-four hides, sixteen skeletons, and fifty-one skulls. Taxidermy was a nineteenth-century way of preserving the buffalo.

Our heroes accumulated money and power, and were willing to use everything up and cause any disturbance. Endless ruination was visited on the land, indigenous people were left to lives of impossible poverty, and the money and power went off to the East. The West was left with stumpage, riparian damage, and holes in the ground. Good people thought it was what you had to do if you wanted to survive; maybe it was. But they left a lot of wreckage. From the gold fields to the petroleum exploration of the early 1980s, the West has continually suffered the whims of a boom-and-bust export economy. Western politics has always been driven by that fact. And, just as importantly, by the warfare between working stiffs and corporations.

On one of my first trips into Montana, I stopped off the highway in the deep-shaft mining town of Wallace, Idaho. The once-upon-a-time elegant hotel barroom was empty except for the heavy-shouldered man down the line a few stools; his legs had been amputated above the knee. "What I got for it," he said, "was notched."

He was talking about a lifetime given to the mines, and he was furious; he grasped the bar with his huge broken-fingered hands, lifted himself, and started coming after me like a crab, suspended on those terrible, quivering forearms, tattoos knotting, his anger so justifiable and futile.

Butte was the empire city of Western mining, a fiefdom of the copper monopoly called the Anaconda Gold and Silver Mining Company. In the early days ore was reduced on charcoal fires in open-hearth smelters; the city lived under toxic yellow smoke. Silicosis was epidemic. A carbide lamp ignited pilings in the Speculator Mine and the shaft became a roaring downdraft chimney; 164 miners died. The Metal Mine Workers' Union organized; fifteen thousand workers in Butte, Anaconda, and Great Falls went on strike. In August of 1917 Frank Little was dragged down a railroad track to a trestle on the outskirts of Butte and hanged by "parties unknown." There was a message pinned to his shirt. "Others take notice. First and last warning." Little had been an agitator for the Wobblies (the International Workers of the World). By 1921 Butte had been under martial law six times.

Visit old women and retired hard-rock miners in Butte, and try to imagine the courage it took to go down seven thousand feet into the terrible darkness of the deep shafts, shift after shift (or the hearts of women who lived their lives with such men). My favorite Butte taverns are the Helsinki, near the Berkeley Pit (the open-pit mine at the edge of town, an enormous toxic waterhole at present), where they send drinks down to the sauna on a dumbwaiter, and the M & M Cigar Store, where waitresses color their hair and fingernails green on St. Patrick's Day.

Westerners learn to suspect the motives of monied outsiders, and take care of the home folks first. Politicians are careful to show concern about the well-being of wage-earning citizens. Sales taxes are widely understood as ways of preying on the poor.

Our traditional sources of income have been shipping timber, minerals, and farm and ranch products to the East. As part of the package Montana suffered vast ecological damage. Our timber is mostly logged, our mines are closing, our farmers and ranchers are suffering sad economic times, and we're engaged in debate as to which of our roadless areas should be dedicated to wilderness and which should be left for logging.

In the fall, when larch on the evergreen slopes turn golden along with the leaves of aspen and cottonwood, visit the logging country along the Bull River in Montana, and talk to the timber fallers and millworkers whose canvas Carhart coveralls are rank with sawdust and sweat. See what they think about attempts to balance the primordial usefulness of nature against their dismay as they face the loss of their jobs, maybe their town.

It's easy to find people to blame for our trouble, but the hue and cry, of which there's more than enough, doesn't solve our problems. People are broke, and being driven to new notions of who they are, and how they might make a living. We know we're privileged to live as we do, with our independence, and freedoms, and we don't want to give them up.

The most viable basis for a reinvigorated economy seems to lie with tourism. It's a concept many Westerners hate. They don't welcome a role in what is essentially "the servant trades." They think their happy land is being turned into a national playground, and zoo.

Locals bemoan the notion that outsiders are buying their way in. Their grievances are no doubt partway an echo of old political lamentations about the division of spoils between the privileged and the poor.

"Them rich people will lock up the gates like they was royalty from Europe," a man told me. "Where the hell will we go hunting?" There's some truth in the notion. But it's more than that—too many people, and their good place will be gone forever, ruined, paved over.

And they are right. People are coming. Our most privileged newcomers are celebrities, and we disdain them but have to admit that many of them are drawn to the West by more than faddism or cowhand chic. They seem to find something in the West that they take to be valuable—the healing usefulness of nature perhaps, escape from the abstract contrivances of our national society—and worth preserving.

But even more than celebrities we are on the receiving end of a stream of retirees and nature freaks and plain citizens interested in a life nearby to wilderness in some approximation of working order, and towns where children can be safe on the streets after school. Maybe they want to sleep with their doors unlocked and open to the summer night, or develop an ongoing relationship with a stretch of trout stream, going to it over seasons until they know the runs and swirls better than they know the lines in their hands. Maybe they want to hike to lakes in high mountains on Friday nights after work in the summertime, and drift to sleep while loons call in the moonlight. Maybe they love the huge banks of lilac blooming beside their house in late spring, busy with hummingbirds.

Maybe they want to live in community with citizens who are well-intentioned toward one another, a place like Augusta, on Elk Creek just upstream from its conjunction with the Sun River just east of the Rockies Front, where the prairies begin. I used to go there in late June, for the rodeo, when the great cottonwoods are in full leaf over the short grassy trail from the single block of downtown stores and taverns to the arena. World champion cowboys fly in to compete with locals. You see their aircraft landing on the meadowland airstrip not far away. They ride in Augusta in the afternoon, fly out and ride that night under the arc lights in some other town, like Cody, Wyoming. I liked to sit near the chutes, where the mud flies. But people say rodeo is another of the animal-taunting sports, like cockfighting, and there seems to be some truth in the notion. So I don't go anymore. Nobody misses me. People in Augusta don't care much about my bicoastal anxieties.

Maybe our newcomers want to hunt pheasants along fence lines in the fall, ski in the immaculate wintertime mountains, or engage in some simple talk of the beauty of things with neighbors they encounter in the barber shop. Maybe they want to take part in politics with some clear sense their efforts could make a difference.

Down in the elegant pasturelands of the Bitterroot Valley there's a yellow nineteenth-century mansion with white trim and beveled windows and a wide veranda. I imagine mowing the lawn beside the sod-banked creek, mopping my forehead with a linen handkerchief, sipping a glass of iced tea, at ease in my kingdom, musing on golf in the afternoon and a raft trip down the river, wine, friends, a few trout for dinner. I dream of the single-hearted heaven that is the coherent self.

Early one summer the people who live in that house were giving a party for children. Red and blue and green helium-filled balloons were floating against the yellow-painted ceiling above the veranda, bobbing in a breath of air. Farmer boys and girls in party dresses were bouncing on a trampoline beside what looked to be an acre of blooming flowers.

Such serenities can lead us to believe we have located a place where serious harm might never come. We wonder if it is possible to get away with enjoying some major percentage of our lives in this good place.

The answer seems to be yes, if we take care, and more care, all of us.

In the West we're living through a transitional time, urgently yearning to inhabit a story that will bring a sensible order into our lives, a story that can only evolve through an almost literally infinite series of recognitions of what we hold to be invaluable. Some of us hope to reinvent the objectives of our society. We've had enough with the irreparable damage. We yearn to engineer the birth of a nation in the West, a heartland empire along the spine of the continent from the blue Canadian Rockies to the cowboy kingdoms in Wyoming and Nevada, and beyond to the ski lift highlands above Durango and Santa Fe, and into the southwestern deserts where the Hopi and citizens at Acoma built their homes on mesa tops in the sky.

The Politics of Storytelling

We continue to inhabit an age of sacred beasts, even as we destroy them. Some of them are ourselves. That's an implied story, complete with recognitions.

Mythologies and community stories shape societies. A mythology is a story that contains implicit instructions from a society to its members, telling them what is valuable and how to conduct themselves if they are to preserve the things they cherish. (I've been thinking about and trying to define the social functions of mythologies and stories since those Sun Valley conferences in the late 1970s—while much of this was written for *Owning It All* and for a variety of magazine pieces in the early 1990s, it was reworked for *Who Owns the West?* and again here.)

The poet C. K. Williams once came to Missoula and spoke of "narrative dysfunction" as a prime part of mental illness in our time. Many of us, he said, lose track of the story of ourselves, which tells us who we are supposed to be and how we are supposed to act. It doesn't just happen to people, it happens to entire societies (for instance, in the United States during the Vietnam War). Stories are places to inhabit, inside the imagination (and places are understood in terms of stories). We all know a lot of stories and we're in trouble when we don't know which one is ours. Or when the one we inhabit doesn't work anymore, and we stick with it anyway.

We live in stories. What we are is stories. We do things because of what is called character, and our character is formed by the stories we learn to live in. Late in the night we listen to our own breathing in the dark, and rework our stories, and we do it again the next morning, and all day long, before the looking glass of ourselves, reinventing our purposes. Without storytelling it's hard to recognize ultimate reasons why one action is more essential than another.

Aristotle talks of "recognitions," which can be thought of as moments of insight or flashes of understanding in which we see through to coherencies in the world. We are all continually seeking such experiences. It's the most commonplace thing human beings do after breathing. We are like detectives, each trying to define what we take to be the right life. It is the primary, most incessant business of our lives.

We figure and find stories, which can be thought of as maps or paradigms in which we see our purposes defined, then the world drifts and our maps don't work anymore, paradigms fail, and we have to reinvent our understandings, and our reasons for continuing. Useful stories, I think, are radical in that they help us see freshly. That's what stories are for, to help us see, and reinvent ourselves.

If we ignore the changing world, and stick to some story too long, we are likely to find ourselves in a great wreck. It's happening all over the American West, right now, to many of us and our neighbors, as we attempt to live out rules derived from an outdated model of society. Old stories, for instance the one about radical independence that is so beloved out

West (and semi-nonsensical in light of our colonial status), are attractive because they tell us we are living the right life.

But they also reconfirm our prejudices. Through them we get to see what we want to see. They may provide consolation but it is not consolation we need. We need clear, fresh insight; we need coherent purposes, intentions. We need to know what we're up to, and exactly why.

The teaching story we grew up with in the West is a pastoral about agricultural ownership (the harvest motif was a rationale for both logging and mining). It's a story that begins with a vast innocent continent, untouched by human and thus natural (actually, it can be more accurately thought of as a garden that was managed, through selective harvesting and wildfires, by the Indians). It's a story about a continent that was alive and capable of inspiring reverence and awe, and yet savage, a wilderness.

It's about rural folk who come from the East, take the land from its native inhabitants, tame it for use, and bring to it a notion of how to live embodied in law (civilization). As old as invading armies, a racist, sexist, imperialist mythology of conquest, it's a rationale for violence against others ("ethnic cleansing") and against what we call nature ("weeding"), the weave of biosystems we inhabit.

That mythology is a lens through which many Westerners continue to see themselves. They like to imagine themselves as honest yeomen who sweat and work in the woods or mines or fields for a living. And many of them are, living in extended families and a work-centered society. They like to think of themselves as people with the good luck and sense to live in a place where a vestige of a natural world still exists in sort of working order. Many incessantly dream of a golden age before fur trappers and deep-shaft miners and cattle barons and logging corporations, computer technocrats and retirees and movie companies, before waves of invasion by what are considered armies of the night.

But nostalgic dreams are always halfway wrong. It's obvious we live in a partway plundered world. Westerners are coming to understand that the West is exploited, threatened by greedy outsiders who want to strip and degrade their sacred place. They hate it.

We incur natural responsibilities. We are responsible for an accurate naming of the world—as it glows in the light and hides in the darkness, as it reeks and breeds, looks, smells and feels, and is known by farmers, cowhands, miners, young women out bow hunting, lovers and loggers, scientists, as it is perceived by creatures, as its systems work, as we are part of them. It's a way to love the world, proclaiming that it is to be preserved and cherished. We need to know what we mean when we say "sacred." But how to proceed?

We must take all the care we can as we try to say what we mean. Debates about "nature" and "wilderness" and "wildness" and "the environment" are critical in our time. It's obvious we should have a secure sense of what people think we mean to say as we use such words. What does it clarify to say "the biosphere is sacred?" Who knows what we mean? Thoreau claimed "wildness" was invaluable. He seems to have been talking about a quality in the "world," and about human responsiveness, and receptiveness, willingness to incorporate, to be part of other things.

Wildness can be thought of as a way of proceeding, a methodology, a way of focusing our attentions (we could call it a state of mind if that metaphor did not imply such stasis). When Thoreau said "wildness," I think he was naming an ability that he found to be supremely valuable, and useful, a confident surrender that facilitates willing release into the possibility of falling (in love? or into acceptance of our fallible, dying situation?).

The notion is both sexual and religious. It's what I've learned to think Thoreau meant by "wildness," a place in the mind, a state of being where I want to go when I am tired of my anxious distancing stupidities, to "wildness," willingness in the self.

From there I have a chance of connecting to the energies of "nature" or "life," which I take to be "sacred." Naming is an attempt to fix processes in place, and hold them static. But processes are what's actual, and won't hold still. Verbs are real, not nouns. We have to incessantly falsify in order to sift the processes we encounter through our scrim of subject-verb-object language.

We must acknowledge the fact that words don't

name, and things don't exist; processes exist, and words evoke. Does that mean we need some kind of new language, no nouns, only verbs, a language in which we can talk about nothing but process inside process?

Arguments about the meaning of words like "nature" and "wilderness" and "wildness" seem to me to be potentially endless. Words denote both concepts and the infinitely complex systems of energy behind the concepts. "Nature" is both a construct and something actual, out there evolving. Constructs and actuality each qualify our sense of the other. Nobody cares if I'm comfortable with that notion, it's simply true.

Narratives try to avoid this problem by inciting us toward making up our own complex, constantly reforming stories out of what has been told, inviting us to look into the mirrors of own selves, and form our own complex and mostly unnamed value systems out of responses to what we experience. In this way narrative attempts to avoid coercion, which is of course a political objective.

Down by the slaughterhouse my grandfather used to keep a chicken wire cage, mounted on a sled so it could be towed off and cleaned, for trapping magpies. His cage worked on the same principle as a lobster trap. The iridescent black-and-white birds could get in to feed on the intestines of butchered cows but they couldn't get out. Those magpies would flutter around in futile exploration, then give in to a sullen acceptance of their fate, hopping around picking at leftovers and waiting.

My grandfather was Scots-English, a very old man by then, but his blue eyes never turned watery and lost. He was one of those deadset desert men, heedless of most everything outside his playground, which was livestock and property, a game that could be called accumulation. But the notes were paid off. You might think he would have been secure, and released to ease back in wisdom. No such luck. He had to keep proving his ownership. This took various forms, like endless litigation, which I have heard described as the sport of kings. But the manifestation I recall most vividly was killing magpies.

About once a week, when a number of magpies were gathered in his trap, maybe ten or fifteen, my grandfather would get out his lifetime 12-gauge shotgun and have someone drive him down to the slaughterhouse in his dusty gray Cadillac, look over his catch, and get down to the business at hand. Once there, the ritual was slow and dignified, and always as inevitable as one shoe after the other.

My grandfather would sit there in his Cadillac, gazing at the magpies with his merciless blue eyes. The magpies would stare back with their hard black eyes. The old man would sigh, and swing open the door on his side of the Cadillac, and climb out, dragging his shotgun behind him, the pockets of his gray gaberdine suit coat bulging with shells. The shotgun stock had been broken, and was wrapped with fine brass wire that shone golden in the sunlight while my grandfather thumbed shells into the magazine. All this without saying a word.

In the ear of my mind I want to imagine the radio playing softly in the Cadillac, something like "Room Full of Roses" or "Candy Kisses," but there was no radio. There was just an ongoing hum of insects, and the clacking of the mechanism as the old man pumped a shell into the firing chamber.

He would lift the shotgun, sight down a barrel with the bluing mostly worn off, into the eyes of those magpies, and then kill them one by one, taking his time, maybe so as to prove this as no accident. After an explosion of feathers and blood, the booming of the shotgun echoing through the flattening light, the old man would mutter, "Bastards." Then he'd take his time killing another.

Finally he would be finished, and turn without looking back, and climb in his side of the Cadillac, where the door still stood open, ready to ride back up the willow-lined lane through the meadows to the ranchhouse, and the cool living room where he would finish out his day playing pinochle with my grandmother and anyone else he could gather, once in a while taking a break to retune the Zenith Trans-Oceanic radio.

No one knew any reason why the old man hated magpies with such specific intensity in his old age. "Where's the difference?" I asked him once.

"Because they're mine," he said. I never did know exactly what he was talking about, the remnants of entrails left after butchering, or the magies.

But it was clear he was claiming absolute lordship over both, and me too, so long as I was living on his property.

We believed we owned the territory, morally and absolutely. We owned it because of our history. Our ancestors brought law to a difficult place, they suffered and shed blood and survived. They had earned this land for us. Their efforts surely earned the right to absolute control. We could do as we saw fit. East of Warner, we summered cattle on a million acres of Taylor Grazing Land, lava rock and sagebrush deserts, country where we owned most of the water, a few acres around each seep spring. But really, we owned it all, or so we felt. Government was distant as news on the radio. Western history has been one resettlement after another, haunted by dreams of possession.

For my grandfather's life and most of mine the idea of property as absolute seemed like a law of nature, even though it never was. But that old folkway, call it a dream, is pretty much irrevocably dead. Many Westerners feel something invaluable has been lost, and they are angered by its going. But, in our best minds, we know that things have always been like this, changing. It's hard to imagine that any man will ever again think he owns the birds.

Truth is, we never own anything absolutely or forever. As our society becomes more and more complex and interwoven, our entitlements become less and less absolute, increasingly likely to be legally diminished. Our rights to property will never take precedence over the needs of society. Nor should they, we must agree in our grudging hearts. Owner-ship of property is always a privilege, granted by so-ciety, and revocable. (This story, and the theorizing at the end, were designed to follow my comments about mythology, and were included in *Owning It All*.)

A few years ago I went back to Warner with a couple of filmmakers from NBC. Footage ran on the *Today Show*. Sitting in an antique GMC pickup truck alongside a great reef of chemically contaminated cowshit that had been piled up outside the feedlot pens where fattening cattle existed like creatures in a machine, I found it in myself to say the valley should be given back to the birds, and turned into a wildlife refuge.

It was a way of saying good-bye. I was saying the biological health of the valley was as important to me as the well-being of the community of ranchers who lived there. I had gone to grade school with some of them. People in Warner mostly understood that act as a betrayal. Some eggs were broken, but I had at last gotten myself to say what I believed.

One Sunday, while living in the heart of the French Quarter of New Orleans during the winter of 1991, Annick and I were out walking in the rain when we realized we were hearing the echoes of someone singing, a vivid unaccompanied voice in the narrow street, maybe three blocks away when I first heard her, a black woman with her eyes closed and face open to the mist as her voice rose and fell to "Glory, Glory, Hallelujah."

She shone in the gray light. I almost couldn't look, and wondered if she cared what anybody thought as I dropped two folded paper dollars into the coffee can at her feet. She didn't look at me. Everything was carpentered. My shuttered door was one in a wall of shuttered doors. The light seemed to rebound from the walls, illuminating wet bricks.

I can still hear that woman. Her life looked to be endlessly more difficult than mine. Her courage and passion were evident in singing even if it was a street hustle for money, and I envied her. I felt like weeping, for myself, and I was afraid of it, like something in my body might break.

There I was, living nearby to some of the best eating and drinking and music in the world, in a place where I never heard so many people—black, white, Creole, Cajun—laughing so much of the time, and I was awash with sadness.

Maybe it was because I had never lived so close to so much violence, which was the other side of things. During Mardi Gras, on Rampart Street, a little more than three blocks from our door, some lost tourist was shot every night, killed and robbed. Every week or so there was a schoolyard killing. Perpetrators in these crimes were often young men from the "projects," public-owned housing for the poor. Those young men were alienated and angry because they saw correctly that their situation in society was hopeless—they were essentially uneducated, their schools were war zones, and their chances of finding jobs, much less meaningful and respected work, were nil. A friend who grew up in New Orleans said, "They've got no place to go. There's no ladder up, no ladder out. They're left with nothing but selfishness. It's the second lesson you learn on the streets." The first lesson, according to my friend, is that nobody is bulletproof.

We should consider the ways the projects, in their capacity to generate hopelessness, are so much like many of our failing towns and our Indian reservations. We should consider the rage generated by disenfranchisement, and the way it looks when it gets to the streets.

The process starts with broken promises. In the West, people came thinking they had been promised something, at least freedom and opportunity, and the possibility of inventing a new, fruitful life. That was the official mythology. When that story didn't come true, the results were alienation and anomie. When people are excluded from what their society has defined for them as the main rewards of life, when they sense that they are absolutely out of the loop, as a lot of Americans do, in the rural outback, and in the deep heartlands of the cities, they sometimes turn to heedless anger. A lot of people on our streets are staring back at us (the enfranchised) with hatred that we all know to be at least partway justifiable. Fewer and fewer of them are willing to stand singing in the rain, waiting for a few dollars to accumulate in the tin can at their feet.

Many of us live with a sense that there is something fundamentally wrong with our society. Many feel our culture has lost track of the reasons why one thing is more significant than another. We are fearful and driven to forget basic generosities. We anesthetize ourselves with selfishness. Many live insulated lives, as I do much of the time. In New Orleans I liked to walk down a couple of blocks to the Bombay Club and disassociate my sensibilities with one and then another huge perfect martini. In Las Vegas I like to stay at the brilliantly named Mirage, amid those orchids and white tigers. What I don't like to do is walk the streets and look the other side of my society in the eye. I want to think I deserve what I get. I don't want to consider how vastly I am overrewarded, or think of the injustices around me. I don't want any encounters with the disenfranchised. I want to say it is not my fault.

But it is, it's mine, and ours. We'd better figure out ways to spread some equity around if we want to go on living in a society that is at least semifunctional. It's a fundamental responsibility to ourselves.

We inhabit a complex culture that is intimately connected to societies all over the world, vividly wealthy while increasingly polarized between rich and poor, increasingly multi-ethnic and multiracial, predominantly urban, sexually ambiguous, ironic, self-reflexive, drugged-up and dangerous and resounding with discordant energies, a selfish inhumane society without a coherent myth to inhabit, a society coming unglued, a democracy that is failing. Many citizens do not believe in it anymore, they don't vote, they withdraw from the processes of governing themselves. On C-Span, all day long, we see the other end of that society, privileged long-faced citizens trying to figure out what to do about our global troubles without forgoing their privileges. We see a society without much idea of how to proceed.

In the United States, the Index of Social Health in the mid-1990s hit its lowest point ever in six categories. They are: (1) Children living in poverty, (2) Child abuse, (3) Health care coverage, (4) Average weekly earnings, (5) Out-of-pocket health care for the elderly, and (6) The gap between rich and poor. We are developing a world society increasingly split into vast hordes of the disenfranchised, and an elitist "first world."

There are millions of ecohomeless people in sub-Saharan Africa, wandering, starving people who'd be coming after us—the most privileged society in history—if they had the strength, and who could blame them? What are we going to do in the future, build nuclear fences?

A society that defines selfishness as a main way of proceeding is embracing both heedlessness and irresponsibility. That so, it can be considered quite literally sociopathic. Good societies work on a sense of mutual affection, which is ordinary in our species.

Citizens in such societies think of responsibilities, then of rewards, which tend to come from a sense of giving, not taking. Insisting on fairness, call it justice, is a way we preserve ourselves and take care of our communities, our kind, thus enhancing our chances at life.

It would help if we could lower our defenses, stop trying to conquer aspects of wildness that frighten us, and admit and follow our passion to care, for nature and for each other. If we want to be happy we should learn to be generous and give the self away (remembering that we cannot take care of any other being or thing until we have taken care of ourselves). We should admit that we want to protect each other; we should admit that we are driven to make a positive effect in the world while staying aware that our notions of positive often derive from our fear of isolation rather than a yearning to take care (Hitler was moved by a racist dream of community).

The weave of interdependent physical, biological, and psychic elements that constitute life is a system of literally unimaginable complexity. We evolved inside those processes; they are under our skins, and in more than metaphoric ways; they are what we are; we are utterly dependent on them, physically and psychically.

"Nature," however we name it, can be wrecked; we are wrecking it; business as usual is madness, and suicidal. We must cherish the evolving processes of life on earth as if they were part of our flesh and soul, because they are; despite all the science fiction about cities in space, nature is our only possible home.

Many of us, by our various means, seek ways to stop that devastation. We think we are trying to save the world for others, and for our children, which is a way of saving ourselves. This is an enterprise, we obviously think, of the uttermost urgency. What to do? How to start?

Our duty, as the dominant species, is to preserve tracts of earth in something like their native condition. The biological interactions necessary to ensure the continuities of life are astonishingly complex and don't take place on islands of semiwilderness.

We yearn to believe that our lives are significant, and that we live in constant, intimate connection to what I can only name as holiness, the invaluable. Without such connection we go increasingly crazy.

We know that it is good for our sanity, as individuals and as a species, to witness evolution operating in multitudinous ways, cells multiplying until a child exists. Involvement with biological complexity helps us feel connected to possibility and meaningfulness. Solace.

Yet, we go on with our involvement in an ecocatastrophe—devastation of the interwoven life on our planet. The only environment in which our species will ever be able to live is withering; maybe "dying" is the word. Today is the most critical moment of the 3½-billion-year history of life on earth. Our lovely home is vanishing, suffering deforestation, desertification, acid rain and radioactive fallout, pesticides and industrial contamination. The result is the destruction of species, from the charismatic (lions, grizzly bears, buffalo, and elephants) to as-yet unnamed beetles. E. O. Wilson tells us that loss of genetic diversity "is the folly our descendants are least likely to forgive us." I'd guess he's correct.

On November 18, 1992, the Union of Concerned Scientists, an international body of academicians and heads of scientific agencies, issued a statement titled "World Scientists' Warning to Humanity." The statement noted that the signers of this declaration included 99 out of the 196 living Nobelists. The essence of their message was this: "No more than one or two decades remain before the chance to avert the threats we now confront will be lost and the prospects for humanity immeasurably diminished." The silence after this plea was profound. We as a society seem unable to respond, unable to imagine anything except business as usual; our politicians for the most part ignore these problems, perhaps hoping they will go away.

We're in a great battle to preserve what's evolved, so it can continue evolving. Our communities, bodies, selves, and systems of ideas must constantly evolve, like any living thing, or they will perish. Business as usual won't do. We can't rely on future technologies to solve our problems.

Why have we been so incapable of responding? Are we simply afraid to look, like flightless birds with their heads in the sand? Not, I think, altogether.

A lot of the problem has to do with the power of huge social entities, government bureaucracies and corporations, and the remarkably similar ways their various methods and conduct work out in the lives of citizens. Westerners look for Shane to come riding out of the Tetons. Instead we get Exxon and the Bureau of Reclamation. One looks as alien as the other.

Corporate and government bureaucracies are formed by people who band together and work toward mutual purposes. They do a lot of good in the world—they distribute food to the poor, they run hospitals. I owe my life to the efficiencies of such organizations. But entrenched bureaucracies tend to insist on projects that are semireal and waste our time, thus implying that our lives are of little value.

Business corporations tend to operate in an atmosphere of institutionalized selfishness; they seldom own up to any debt except to their stockholders and show little interest in moral responsibility. They use the power of their funds to manipulate government, buy up media, and manipulate information, lying incessantly.

In the American West angry people talk of rebellion against local and federal governments. They want to get power into the hands of locals, and that sounds good. But how then do we control corporate powers? The entities that buffer ordinary citizens against the corrosive selfishness of corporations are our bureaucracies. And on around the circle of love. How can we reinvent the laws that determine the ways both bureaucratic and economic power are allowed to function in our world society?

Our task is to be smart as we can manage and try to get smarter, and to follow our passion to be decent. Our job is to keep on trying to name and rename those things we take to be sacred (like nature) and to honor them. In that way we may come to the luck of having spent our lives inside the solace of a coherent self at large in a coherent world, a situation in which one by one we work at that complex thing, which is being decent to one another, and decent to things.

Fully imagined and precisely rendered storytelling about creatures and communities, human and otherwise, in the so-called "natural" world can lead us to the once-upon-a-time quite commonplace but now rarer pleasure of inhabiting a sense that we are irrevocably wedded into electric processes of what is actual, that we are participants in the system of energies in which we feel whole. We intuit that we are part of holiness. We must reinforce that intuition. We need a story about compassion and caretaking that is so compelling people will act it out as they work and vote. Our story will center on our need to cherish ourselves and our primordial situation.

Finding that story, increment by increment, is our most urgent communal enterprise. That story, when found, will be a gift, passing from one person to another. And then our institutions will change, almost at once.

Belief

Paradise, it is said, is all around us. Can we not see it? How do we make sense of that thought? Incessant suffering is everywhere and will always continue, life being what it is. How to name those aspects of existence that are most valuable? Freedom, justice, love—what do we mean? How to define ourselves?

We are animals evolved to be at home among other animals. Our ancestors lived with dreams of animal companions. The great bears vanished into caves, and came out when the snows were melted. Watching bears, and plants budding and flowering, people imagined the chance of reemerging into life after death, renewal and some variety of resurrection.

Carl Sagan wrote, "Electricity is the way nature behaves." Which is true. Electricity is actual. The "natural" world is something we create in our imaginations, out of sensory experience filtered through language. Places, to the degree we can know them, are locations for stories about significances we've found there. They are also our only home.

Human cultures build on accumulated information. Rather than biologically adapt to environments, we've learned to use our powers of invention to refit the various places we live. People plant seeds, lead water to crops, wait out summer for the harvest; they breed animals for slaughter, learn despair, harden their hearts, cultivate intimacy by promenading the marketplace, practice sex on the beach, garden, build cities, run our routes, advertise, and accumulate. We learn to think of ourselves in the third person, to talk about ourselves as if we were objects, to be self-reflexive, think about thinking and even wonder if we are imaginary. And maybe we are, creatures made of imagining. We've distanced ourselves from the situation in which we evolved through what I take to be the processes of learning to think.

We've structured our organizational ideologies from inside isolations. Contemporary churches, states, corporations, and bureacracies are energized by a weave of stories about using and ownership, for instance stories like the one about Hemingway hiring boys to trap magpies in Sun Valley one summer so he and Gary Cooper could have live targets for their shotgun practice, part of the poetry of slaughter. Societal organizing stories could just as easily be about gifts and generosity.

But we have to struggle to name things we won't relinquish, like compassion or old-growth forest or high times on Saturday night; we want to be done with cold-heartedness and the empty-pocket blues; we want transcendent mornings, turkey dinners with old pals, and sweet singing later on. We yearn to be at ease with our animal selves, we love the joys of fathoming what and where we are, and we long to make responsible use of what we know. What to do, how to act? How to honor our obligations to the processes of joyousness? We might start with gifts. Maybe generosity could become habitual. It's my theory that everyone yearns, as we did in Warner, plowing those swamps, with all that bulldozing, to make a positive effect in the world. But how?

We kill to eat. How to mitigate the guilt? Is that what we're trying to do, as we tell ourselves what to grieve for and celebrate? We are many-headed, our minds full of witnesses, without spontaneity. Self-consciously, we try to teach ourselves to work at generosity. Solace lies, if anywhere, in the details and complexities we are part of, weather swirling in recognizable patterns, and the colors, browns and greens against the blue—you can lie down in the grass. It's what we have. If there's an art to being human and comfortable, part of it involves learning to get quiet. We know the rituals of gentleness and intimacy. Play, wisdom says, with those you love.

These are things I believe:

- Everything is part of everything.
- Destroying life, or the possibility of life, is a way of destroying ourselves, eating ourselves alive.
- We are irrevocably communal. Our communities are living parts of what we are. Destroy them, and we begin destroying ourselves.
- We are responsible for taking care of all life on the planet, our only possible home.
- Our consequent political agenda involves rethinking ultimate purposes. Otherwise, down the road we're traveling at present, we're going to be deep in the soup, dead in the water, cooked.
- Generosity, I think, is the prime moral and political virtue.

- And compassion. We have no choice but to forgive ourselves.

These ideas are pretty simple. The trickiness resides, of course, in the working out, and making do. How to keep from doing harm? Sometimes that seems to be the only question. To an increasing degree, human cultures are free from the workings of physical evolution. Our thinking centers on evolving ideas. But we have to act. To do so responsibly we must first examine, with all possible rigor, our desires. What do we really want?

My beliefs, if they are beliefs, feel like dreams. What a peculiar thing—naming beliefs. There's no methodology. Beliefs are like air, and maybe never justifiable; they are the medium we live in.

Ray Carver sent me a copy of the last book he published in his lifetime, *Where I'm Calling From,* inscribed "with abiding friendship." It came a week before he died. Which meant it had been inscribed by a man who knew he was on the runway while the rest of the world was off somewhere having fun.

In my sixth decade, friends dying, I have not come to anything like a set of consolations for my own fragility. It is no joking matter. Irreligious as a stone, I'm no more profound or coherent in my thinking about such matters than I was at age eleven. Let it go, I thought (at eleven), there's plenty of time, you'll think of something.

But no such luck. Soon enough I am going to have my chance. It's time to lay hands on a sustaining mythology. If I were dying, would I be inconsolable? How do you get consolable? I tell myself I had better find a way.

Purple and white lilac blossom in enormous actual clots of splendor along alleyways in Missoula. Aren't they enough? I pull on knee-high rubber boots and head across the meadows behind the log house where Annick lives on spring mornings after the snows melt and run-off comes, and walk along splashing in the water. Amid blooming daisies and wild roses I shovel up dams in the sodded ditches, working water along a ridge of high ground. It's a try at directing flow in the world. I crouch close and taste the sour stink of growth, watch long-legged insects walk the water, and I am home again.

When people ask if I don't feel a terrible sense of loss, cut off from the valley and methods of my childhood, I tell them no. I don't own a square inch of land, haven't for decades, and I feel no need to. The world is there anyway. But maybe I'm spoiled. Maybe I got the need to own things out of my system at an early age. Nothing much looks to have changed when I go back to Warner. The rim is black against the sunset light, as it was when I was a child. The apple trees, where I climbed, still blossom. Think of *familia*, hearth and home fire, the fishing creek falling out of the mountains, into the valley, the Lombardy poplar beside the white house, and the orchard where children run in deep sweet clover under the blossoming apple trees. That's my paradise, the garden of my childhood. The topography of my dreams, I like to think, is mostly intact.

What would a paradise on earth be like? Start with a process, I think, with everybody involved, taking part in the reimagining, thinking up the land of our heart's desiring, how things could be if cherishing were our main concern. Think of it as a story that could be lived, a sensible plot that could be acted out.

On warm afternoons in Missoula the autumn sky can be blue-white and infinite in its distance from our concerns. The needles off the larch in the high country will have gone golden, falling like glory on the logging roads. Cottonwood along the rivers bloom yellow and huge against evergreen mountains, and in that little eternity we're untouchable. We will never grow old; our people will never die. No one will break into our house while we're gone.

Too much order and artificiality makes us crazy. The feel of mud where the leeches breed, as it oozes around my ankles, and osprey fishing with their killing clarity of purpose, all the stink and predatory swiftness of things, are part of what I understand as most valuable. Seacoasts can be heart-stopping, a melding of aspects both actual and imagined that draws us to intuit that actuality does not proceed in haphazard ways even if it is a fiction, a way of imagining that says our time and stories are not meaningless.

We want luminous significances to inhabit the story of our life. We yearn to live in a place we can name, where we can feel safe. We want that place to exist like a friend, somebody we understand intimately. We want stories that reassure us in our sense that we deserve to be loved. We want the story of our lives to have a sensible plot. We want it to go somewhere, and mean something.

What we need most urgently is a fresh dream of who we are, which will tell us how we should act, stories about taking care of what we've got, which is to say life and our lives. The story I want to call mine is about justice and taking care, in which my home is sacred, a story about making use of the place where we live without ruining it, which reminds us to stay humane amid our confusions.

We need to inhabit stories that will encourage us toward acts of the imagination, which in turn will drive us to the arts of empathy, for each other and the world. We need stories that will encourage us to understand we are part of everything, that the world exists under our skins, and that destroying it is a way of killing ourselves. We need stories that will drive us to care for one another, all the creatures, stories that will drive us to take action. We need stories that will tell us what kind of action to take.

We need stories that tell us reasons why compassion and the humane treatment of our fellows is more important—and interesting—than feathering our own nests as we go on accumulating property and power. Our lilacs bloom, and buzz with honeybees and hummingbirds. We can still find ways to live in some approximation of home-child heaven.

We have to acknowledge that we are animals, and understand that the living world cannot be replicated. We hear pipe dreams about cities in space, but it is clearly impossible to replicate the infinite complexities of the world in which we have evolved. Wreck it and we will have lost ourselves, and that is craziness. We evolved to live in the interpenetrating energies and subjectivities of all the life there is so far as we know, which coats the rock of earth like moss. We cannot live without connection, both psychic and physical. We begin to wither in isolation even if some of us can hang on for a long while connected to nothing beyond our imaginations.

Paradise, to my seeing, my hearing, my smelling, my touch, is unending immersion in the evolving processes of a world where my kind of creature feels both comfortable and meaningful. Imagine summertime rain falling over an alpine meadow. Imagine fireweed, silvery lupine, wood lilies, Indian paintbrush, showy green gentian, pink plumes, clustered penstemon, false hellebore, and butterflies like Weidemeyer's Admiral and great spangled fritillary, globe flowers and western toads and fringed gentian; imagine calliope hummingbirds, sharp-nosed voles, garter snakes and gophers, thunder in the afternoon, faraway lightning, the smell of ozone. Imagining is part of it. Certain Buddhists try to save themselves from sorrow by meditating on a place of their own inventing, which they call Pure Land. They see swirls in the waters of an imagined river, and a make-believe butterfly in the sun, and claim they find peace inside the imagining creature they are. I'm more drawn to some actual return to a version of our ancient situation, a communal garden inside vast thickets of wilderness, the creatures consorting with one another and satisfied. The ultimate question, however complex the working out, is simple enough: How to think up a just and sustaining community for ourselves on this transmogrified planet?

But there is no single story that names paradise. There never will be. Our stories have to be constantly reworked, reseen. Energies and processes are what is actual, complexity is actual. We inhabit thickets of responsibility, and wonder how good we can be. Spinoza said, "Desire and pursuit of the whole is called love." The apparent world resonates with all the meaning there is going to be. That, I believe. *Momento vivere.*

William Kittredge

A PORTRAIT

by Scott Slovic

Driving home from my office the other night, I glanced into a student apartment through an open curtain. Against the bright whiteness of the apartment wall, the room was dominated by an enormous rack of horns, probably the head of a deer. On one of the points hung, nonchalantly, a tan cowboy hat. As I continued home, I asked myself, What could be the sensibility of someone who would use an animal's head as a hat rack?

This willingness to use the planet for our own benefit, this sense that the rest of the material world is inert and unconscious, may well be the pervasive worldview of people living in contemporary industrialized cultures. From Europe to Asia, from country to city, there is evidence of an amoral materialism that determines the use of resources, the choice of lifestyle. Nature has become not a counterlife, a respected other, but dumb *stuff*. Even the literature of nature sometimes appears to be a collection of experiences, pinned to the pages like so many beetles and butterflies.

In this vacuum of morality and magic, modern culture is greatly impoverished—we are suffering a terrible, terrifying loss and in many cases do not even realize it. What we secretly desire may well be what science historian Morris Berman has termed "the reenchantment of the world." No one feels this loss and the accompanying desire for revitalization more profoundly than contemporary nature writers, especially those writers who have actually lived in "paradise" and then seen it go away, perhaps even contributed to its evanescence. Unlike the tale of Eden, the lost paradise of the American West is not a story of exile from the garden, but a confession of destruction, of murdering places brimming with life and beauty. One of the most important tellers of this story is Montana author William Kittredge.

William Kittredge is a storyteller but not a mere entertainer. His stories (both fiction and nonfiction), for the most part, aim to challenge and instruct— the vitality of characters and the beauty of description are not ends in themselves, but tools in service of social reform. Confrontational, confessional, self-critical, regretful, melancholy—these terms easily fit much of Kittredge's writing. He tells stories of cold, dusty towns and sprawling ranchlands and inhospitable, uncharismatic mountain ranges and desperate— sometimes violently desperate—people. There is a feeling of sober realism and embittered social critique in many of the short stories from *We Are Not in This Together* and essays from such books as *Owning It*

All and *Hole in the Sky.* But perhaps the essential idea that motivates Kittredge's work as an author, that defines his attitude toward both art and the western American land, appears in the middle of the title essay of his 1987 book *Owning It All:*

> In the American West we are struggling to revise our dominant mythology, and to find a new story to inhabit. Laws control our lives, and they are designed to preserve a model of society based on values learned from mythology. Only after reimagining our myths can we coherently remodel our laws, and hope to keep our society in a realistic relationship to what is actual.

This statement identifies "mythology"—story with a capital "S"—as the foundation of human values, as the source of what we call worldview. Elsewhere, Kittredge and Steven M. Krauzer have written that "a myth is a message from society to its members, suggesting appropriate behavior and response" and that "it is arguable that the mythology most commonly associated with the American West is the most enduring and influential message our society has given us in the two hundred years of American social history." Everything else in our lives, from technology to law, develops in accordance with the stories we tell ourselves about how we live and how we ought to live, Kittredge argues. Although his own experience is primarily of the intermountain region of the American West, much of what he says is applicable to every region of North America and much of the industrialized world. We are engaged in a struggle to "revise our dominant mythology," and one could argue that this struggle is as endless as it is inevitable. Perhaps it is human nature to dream, to live in a way that corresponds to dreams, and then periodically to wake up and realize how far awry we've gone from what physical reality can support. This is one of the lessons of Malthusian economics, and it's one of the key lessons of William Kittredge's writing. Another lesson is that the physical world is a primary locus of truth and beauty, something to seek and not to fear: "I'm yearning for meaningful contact with the actual," Kittredge states in *Who Owns the West?* This quest, too, is central to his life and work.

The images on my computer monitor flare into color as the cursor moves across the screen, mimicking the motion of a flashlight on a cave wall. I've used the World Wide Web to track down information about the Paleolithic painted caves of Lascaux, France, and have come across a site that depicts a cave in its actual darkness, enabling visitors to shine their cursors upon the ancient walls. I see bulls, bison, horses, various deerlike animals. Although the cave seems lifeless at first, the walls turn out to be teeming with animal life as one moves the cursor—images of animals have been projected by human imaginations into color powders made of iron oxide and manganese bioxyde. Reds, yellows, and blacks. These walls are alive. The imaginations of the people who made these paintings seventeen thousand years ago were also alive. Some have referred to the caves of Lascaux as sanctuaries for the most sacred belongings and ideas of these ancient people: expressions of thanks and devotion to the animals that helped to sustain human life. The animal paintings of Lascaux are eerily tranquil, implying no trauma, no bitterness of mortal struggle. The animals appear autonomous, in control of their own destinies as they traverse the sides of the caves. Never do they turn to look the human observer in the eye.

The first time I met William Kittredge, he and his partner, Annick Smith, had just returned to the United States from a trip to France in March 1995, where they had had the opportunity to view the cave paintings of Lascaux. They routed their return trip to Montana through Dallas, Texas, so that Bill could join a panel called "Landscape in Literature"—along with Texas authors Stephen Harrigan and Elizabeth Crook and fellow Montanan Rick Bass—at the John Graves Day event hosted by the Dallas Museum of Art in honor of the great Texas nature writer. The seventy-year-old Graves, who attended the panel discussion, is himself a writer whose monumental books about rural Texas, such as *Goodbye to a River* and *Hard Scrabble*, exemplify the attentiveness to details of history and physical place that make Kittredge's own work so vivid. Graves wrote in a 1978 lecture:

> A sense of place is bound up to some degree
> with the way people are in that place and with
> the history of the people, and it's bound up
> even more with physical and natural detail,

with trees and grass and soil, creatures, weather, water, sky, wild sounds, the way some weed smells when you walk on it. These are the details of place, and an awareness of them is what I call [a sense of] place.

Introducing the panel on "Landscape in Literature," I felt compelled to draw upon Kittredge's call for contemporary American society to "re-imagin[e] our myths" and find new ways for us "to keep our society in a realistic relationship to what is actual." I asked the panelists if they felt their own work was an attempt to create new guiding myths, and if so, what stories they would like to see our culture come to "inhabit." When it was his turn to speak, Kittredge told the story of his childhood in the remote Warner Valley of southeastern Oregon on a vast ranch of superabundant wildlife, and he told the story of his recent visit to Lascaux and what the lives of the cave painters must have been like for them to depict such animals on the walls of their sanctuaries—and he expressed his desire, by way of literature, to re-imagine contemporary America as a culture in which animals and other natural phenomena would reclaim a central place in our moral and imaginative lives and would, indeed, become physically present and familiar again. In other words, for Kittredge, the goal of the writer is nothing short of revitalizing and revivifying the physical world. In 1992, he told an interviewer, "When I was five or six years old, I stood out on the lawn where I grew up in Warner Valley, on a spring morning, and watched the waterbirds go over, and there were thousands and thousands and thousands, literally. . . . Raft and flock after flock." "Waterbirds," he has explained, "were a metaphor for abundance beyond measure in my childhood."

But in between the moments of rhapsodic memory and visionary mythologizing come spells of despair, of bleak observation. In "Owning It All," he recalls another scene of birds and sky when he was around ten:

> I was watching the waterbirds coming off the valley swamps and grainfields where they had been feeding overnight. They were going north to nesting grounds on the Canadian tundra, and that piece of morning, inhabited by the sounds of their wings and their calling in the clean air, was wonder-filled and magical. I was enclosed in a living place.
>
> No doubt that memory persisted because it was a sight of possibility which I will always cherish—an image of the great good place rubbed smooth over the years like a river stone, which I touch again as I consider why life in Warner Valley went so seriously haywire. But never again in my lifetime will it be possible for a child to stand out on a bright spring morning in Warner Valley and watch the waterbirds come through in enormous, rafting vee-shaped flocks of thousands—and I grieve.

This vacillation between reverie and grief, reformist hope and guilt-ridden despair, defines the overarching tenor of Kittredge's writing. Already in his first published work of nonfiction, a review essay titled "The Snow Never Falls Forever" that appeared in *Harper's* in 1972, he was expressing this profoundly compelling and paradoxical lesson, this "realist nostalgia": "Too many things have been lost. Myths of innocence always point backward, toward simplicities impossible to regain. Yet we need and love them, especially in times as complex and difficult as these."

William "Bill" Kittredge was born in Portland, Oregon, on August 14, 1932. He was raised on a cattle ranch and farm near Lakeview, nearly three hundred miles southeast of Eugene, Oregon, and in another world from the loci of artistic and intellectual life where he would come to spend most of his adulthood. His father, Oscar Kittredge, ran the ranch when Bill was growing up, reveling in the possibility of creating a perfect paradise for industrialized agriculture. The family owned thirty-three square miles of irrigated cropland and controlled the grazing rights to more than fifteen hundred square miles of Great Basin high desert. Oscar Kittredge had grown up on a homestead in the sage-covered plains near the town of Silver Lake. Kittredge recalls that his grandfather bought the MC Ranch in Warner Valley in 1936, with no down payment, when the valley was still mostly swampland. Then began the process of transforming the land, making it pay off:

> The outside work was done mostly by men and horses and mules, and our ranch valley was

filled with life. In 1937 my father bought his first track-layer, a secondhand RD6 Caterpillar he used to build a 17-mile diversion canal to carry the spring floodwater around the east side of the valley, and we were on our way to draining all swamps. The next year he bought an RD7 and a John Deere 36 combine which cut an 18-foot swath, and we were deeper into the dream of power over nature and men, which I had begun to inhabit while playing those long-ago games of war.

This process of achieving ever greater control over the physical environment of the Warner Valley continued for three decades, and eventually chief responsibility for the ranch passed into Bill Kittredge's own hands. In the 1980s, long after he had left the MC Ranch, he began to recount his experiences on the ranch in miscellaneous essays, many of which have since been collected in books. The central articulation of his family's experience on the MC, though, is the essay "Owning It All," with its ironic double entendre that suggests both the mythology of possession and control that dictated the Kittredge family's rural life and the process of confessing (owning up) his misgivings, retrospectively, about that mythology and the lifestyle it engendered. After summarizing the ever-increasing process of dominating nature on the MC Ranch by way of vast irrigation systems and powerful pesticides, Kittredge recalls a car trip through the mountain west with his aging father, during which the two of them reflected on their "dreamland gone wrong" and realized that their mythology of violent domination had given them "enormous power over nature, and a blank perfection of fields." The abiding guilt from his own contribution to this process has led Kittredge to use his writing as a ritual of confession, turning the same stories of domination and degradation into newly woven essays, collages of previous tellings. Absolution, if it comes at all, will appear in the form of social transformation in the American West: in particular, less destructive processes of ranching, farming, hunting, mining, and logging.

Even while Kittredge was learning the rugged outdoor ways of high desert ranching from his father, he began to get inklings "that there was more to life than cattle ranching" from his mother, Josephine (Miessner) Kittredge, the daughter of a power company blacksmith from Klamath Falls, Oregon, who had taken piano and voice lessons and yearned throughout her life to do something in the arts. Kittredge attended high school in Klamath Falls before leaving the ranch for Oregon State College in Corvallis, where he majored in agriculture but began dabbling with writing and in fact received some of his first serious instruction in the art of fiction from novelist Bernard Malamud. He also met his first wife, Janet, in college; they were married in 1951 at the age of nineteen. Their daughter Karen was born in 1954, and their son Bradley two years later. Following his graduation from Oregon State in 1953, Kittredge served in the Air Force from 1954 to 1957, doing stints in San Antonio, Denver, at Travis Air Force Base in northern California, and in Guam. "My plan," he recalled in *Hole in the Sky*,

> was to spend my air force years pursuing my secret life, reading the important books of the world and getting ready to become a writer. But when I actually seated myself before the typewriter my wife had brought to our marriage, a ranch boy with a degree in general agriculture from Oregon State College, the writing was as unreal as the air force. So I gave it up. There was plenty of time. After my time in the service I could go home to Warner Valley. First I would read all the books; then I'd know what to say.

In 1957, Kittredge returned with his family to the Warner Valley to work the family ranch: "I was hot shit, hiring and firing and buying and selling and only twenty-six." But his hands were "soft like a baby's." His father, by this time, had divorced Kittredge's mother, been disinherited from the ranch and farm, and turned to alcohol. Kittredge became "farming boss" at the MC, and did this work for eight years.

It was during his watch that the agricultural paradise of the MC began to fall apart. Again and again, he has told this story: in *Owning It All, Hole in the Sky, Who Owns the West?* and now in this new book, *Taking Care.* He writes:

> We sprayed 2-4-D ethyl and malathion and the World War II German nerve gas called parathion

(for clover mites in the barley), working to shorten our own lives. We baited the coyotes with 1080 and hunted them from airplanes; we wiped them out. The rodent population exploded and field mice destroyed our alfafa [sic]. We irrigated and re-irrigated, pumped and drained; our peat soil began to go saline.

For Kittredge and his family, this agonizing process was like the end of the world. Even after the farming boss and his farmhands began to recognize the decline of the place, they could not figure out how to stay the inevitable: "The ecology of the valley was complex beyond our understanding, and it began to die as we went on manipulating it in ever more frantic ways. As it went dead and empty of the old life it became a place where no one wanted to live."

The decline of the MC Ranch was accompanied by Kittredge's own psychological fraying. He writes about this in *Hole in the Sky:*

By craziness I mean nearly catatonic fearfulness generated by the conviction that nothing you do connects to any other particular thing inside your daily life. Mine was never real craziness, although some fracturing of the ice seemed to lie just around the corner of each moment; it was easy to imagine vanishing into complete disorientation. My trouble could be called "paralysis in the face of existential realities," a condition I could name, having read Camus like any boy of my time.

Kittredge spent much of the 1960s drinking and womanizing; his marriage with Janet dissolved in 1967, and the family ranch was sold. Thanks in part to his mother's continuing cultural influence, he "had come to worship and yearn for books and ideas," for the cosmopolitan life, although his "yearnings seemed almost perverse. Why couldn't the immediacy of family and work and property be enough?" By 1968, he had married Patty, but this union too was quickly in trouble. After several months studying creative writing at the University of Oregon, he was admitted to the Iowa Writers' Workshop. Despite the shakiness of their marriage, Kittredge could not "imagine going alone" to Iowa and resisted Patty's offer to "call it off right now." She traveled with him to Iowa City and saw him "through the years of disorientation and foolishness attendant on starting up the literary life." After Iowa, Kittredge was offered a teaching position at the University of Montana in Missoula—a position he would hold for nearly thirty years—and he and Patty made their way west again in 1969. He continued to drink, and their marriage continued to falter; by 1974, following a year on a Stegner Fellowship at Stanford, he was ready to break up with Patty. Kittredge began his relationship with Montana author and filmmaker Annick Smith in 1977; he attributes much of his emotional stability and literary productivity for the past two decades to this relationship.

Although Kittredge had published several dozen short stories and a handful of essays by the mid-1970s, his literary career didn't really begin to take off until 1977, when his publishing partnership with Steven M. Krauzer was established. A Missoula resident like Kittredge, the twenty-nine-year-old Krauzer was just launching his career as writer of mysteries, Westerns, action-adventure novels, and screenplays when they began to collaborate. The two of them edited a series of books, including *Great Action Stories, The Great American Detective,* and *Fiction into Film,* between 1977 and 1979, and launched under the pseudonym "Owen Rountree" a nine-book series of coauthored adventure novels called "Cord," emphasizing the Western landscape and frontier experiences; the Cord books appeared between 1982 and 1986. Kittredge has published two collections of his own stories, *The Van Gogh Field and Other Stories* in 1978 and *We Are Not in This Together* in 1984; his fiction emphasizes harsh landscapes and fractured relationships in the intermountain west, from Nevada to Montana. In the late 1970s, he began to develop the essays about his life in Warner Valley that later constituted his first major book of nonfiction, *Owning It All:* "Redneck Secrets," "Overthrust Dreams," "Silver Bullets," "Natural Causes," and "Owning It All" appeared in such periodicals as *Rocky Mountain Magazine, Outside,* and *Pacific Northwest Magazine* before being collected, with other selections, in the 1987 book. Critic Glen A. Love has described *Owning It All* as "a mature and convincing portrait of his owned territory, written with the unmistakable authenticity of the insider who has also managed to get outside."

In 1988, Kittredge teamed up with Annick Smith to edit *The Last Best Place: A Montana Anthology,* a book that has been heralded as the model anthology of its kind. Including traditional Native American tales and myths and accounts by explorers, and working up to contemporary selections from such authors as Thomas McGuane and David Quammen, the monumental volume is 1,161 pages in length. Kittredge and Smith have also worked together on several film projects, and served as coassociate producers for Robert Redford's 1992 *A River Runs Through It.*

In the 1990s, Kittredge published two more books of nonfiction, the memoir *Hole in the Sky* in 1992 and the volume of nonfiction meditations and fragments *Who Owns the West?* in 1996. *Hole in the Sky* is a wrenchingly confessional autobiography, a litany of guilt and regret, of lost opportunities and broken relationships among people and between people and places. The memoir expresses yearning to reconnect with "the intimate particularities of the world we lived in as children" and with an ultimate reality beyond the dreams and desires of the human mind ("If only we could find some trick by which we could be alive without the imagination standing between us and whatever is out there"). Above all, the book is a statement of personal responsibility, a book-length "owning up" of the author's own contribution to the many failures he lists: "We feel so guilty; we know it is all our fault." This last statement might well be what all of us in the American West, directly complicit or not, need to say before we can truly begin the process of mending the ravaged landscapes of this region. Jane Smiley, author of *A Thousand Acres*, commented in her review:

> *Hole in the Sky* is a valuable memoir that should be read with care, for it explores the first American dream, the dream of property that was written into the Declaration of Independence before anyone thought of "the pursuit of happiness" and still stands, for many, as the real American dream. It is a dream that William Kittredge has found false and hollow. His voice should be a prophetic one.

The publication of *Who Owns the West?* heralded an important shift in Kittredge's extended process of owning up/ownership, moving beyond self-flagellation toward conciliation, vision, and love. Much of the book explores the *idea* of "paradise," not merely chronicling the loss of paradise as in the earlier books of nonfiction, but instead speculating about a possible return. Chapter 3 of part 1, "Heaven on Earth," was originally published in *Audubon* under the title "Second Chance at Paradise." Instead of wringing his hands at the past damage, Kittredge points to a state of mind that might help us to avoid repeating the mistakes of the MC Ranch:

> It's time we gave something back to the natural systems of order that have supported us, some care and tenderness, which is the most operative notion, I think—tenderness. . . . We need to give some time to the arts of cherishing the

things we adore, before they simply vanish. Maybe it will be like learning a skill: how to live in paradise.

The possibility of learning this skill marks a significant new optimism in Kittredge's writing, an optimism echoed in the title of *Taking Care,* a book that continues the author's habit of cutting, pasting, and retelling stories from his earlier volumes, including *Who Owns the West?* There is also a newly explicit mention of things spiritual in Kittredge's more recent work, such as these comments that were published in slightly altered form under the title "A Saving Light" in *Outside:* "One of my reasons for living in Montana is the light in October. I was not raised to pay much attention to notions of the sacred, but I think of this light as holy. . . . What I have been seeking, most centrally, is a way to imagine myself healed to the glory of things in this light."

In October 1995, Jack Ward Thomas, chief of the U.S. Forest Service, spoke to a packed auditorium of more than five hundred people on the campus of the University of Montana. He offered platitudes concerning the forest service's goal of mediating between competing interests in American society, chastised the crowd for being unruly, and delicately avoided commenting directly on his agency's role in supporting timber sales in the Pacific Northwest. The organizers of the event had asked Bill Kittredge to follow the forest service chief with ten minutes of comments for the hometown crowd. Kittredge strolled to the microphone looking like a professorial teddy bear with his glasses, curly hair, and barrel chest. But far from pacifying the bored and frustrated audience, he opened by accusing the forest service of being in cahoots with big business and went on directly from there. Each comment elicited a roar of approval from the crowd. Soon everyone in the lecture hall was standing, waiting for the next jab at the Establishment. This was clearly a speaker who had his finger on the pulse of his listeners, who spoke not only for himself but for many of his fellow Westerners.

Bill Kittredge did not set out to become the spokesperson for his region. He began his life as a writer by trying to find an authentic voice and a subject he knew something about, and as he gradually came home to his literary form and subject, he learned that he had a waiting group of readers and listeners: Westerners, urban and rural, who wanted his help in articulating the identity of this vast, varied region during a time of radical transition. Unlike the series of one-line political jabs offered in response to Jack Ward Thomas, Kittredge's typical statements come in the form of narratives. He is, first and foremost, a storyteller—and he takes this as a high calling. His contribution to *The True Subject: Writers on Life and Craft* is a riff titled "Doing Good Work Together" (another version of this is the concluding section of *Who Owns the West?*), which includes the following summary:

We live in stories. What we are is stories. We do things because of what is called character, and our character is formed by the stories we learn to live in. Late in the night we listen to our own breathing in the dark and rework our stories. We do it again the next morning, and all day long, before the looking glass of ourselves, re-inventing reasons for our lives. Other than such storytelling there is no reason to things.

This statement—this entire book—is the "credo" of a storyteller.

Bibliography of William Kittredge's Work

by Scott Slovic

BOOKS

Who Owns the West? San Francisco: Mercury House, 1996.

Hole in the Sky. New York: Knopf, 1992.

Lost Cowboys (But Not Forgotten). New York: Whitney Museum, 1992.

Owning It All. St. Paul: Graywolf Press, 1987.

Phantom Silver. Missoula, Mont.: Kutenai Press, 1987 (limited edition).

With Steven M. Krauzer. *Cord: Brimstone Valley.* New York: Ballantine Books, 1986.

With Steven M. Krauzer. *Cord: Paradise Valley.* New York: Ballantine Books, 1986.

With Steven M. Krauzer. *Cord: Gunsmoke River.* New York: Ballantine Books, 1985.

With Steven M. Krauzer. *Cord: Hunt the Man Down.* New York: Ballantine Books, 1984.

With Steven M. Krauzer. *Cord: Kin of Colorado.* New York: Ballantine Books, 1984.

We Are Not in This Together. Foreword by Raymond Carver. St. Paul: Graywolf Press, 1984.

With Steven M. Krauzer. *Cord: Black Hills Duel.* New York: Ballantine Books, 1983.

With Steven M. Krauzer. *Cord: Gunman Winter.* New York: Ballantine Books, 1983.

With Steven M. Krauzer. *Cord: The Nevada War.* New York: Ballantine Books, 1982.

With Steven M. Krauzer. *Cord.* New York: Ballantine Books, 1982.

The Van Gogh Field and Other Stories. Columbia: University of Missouri Press, 1978.

EDITED BOOKS/JOURNALS

The Portable Western Reader. New York: Penguin, 1997.

Montana Spaces. New York: Nick Lyons Books, 1988.

With Annick Smith. *The Last Best Place: A Montana Anthology.* Helena, Mont.: Montana Historical Society Press, 1988. Seattle: University of Washington Press, 1991.

With Steven M. Krauzer. *TriQuarterly* (Spring 1980), special issue on contemporary Western fiction.

With Steven M. Krauzer. *Fiction to Film.* New York: Harper & Row, 1979.

With Steven M. Krauzer. *The Great American Detective.* New York: New American Library, 1978.

With Steven M. Krauzer. *Great Action Stories.* New York: New American Library, 1977.

STORIES

"Looking Glass." *American Short Fiction* (Fall 1993).

"All Frogs." *Cold Drill* (Spring 1993).

"Sleeping Alone." *Left Bank* (Winter 1992).

"Three Dollar Dogs." *American Short Fiction* (Summer 1991).

"The Coast." *Hayden's Ferry Review* (Spring/Summer 1991).

"Do You Hear Your Mother Talking?" *Harper's* (February 1991).

"Rich." *CutBank* (Spring 1988).

"Cities in the Sky." *Epoch* 36, no. 3 (1988).

"Balancing Water." *Paris Review* (Fall 1987).

"Stoneboat." *Arts Review: National Endowment for the Arts* 4, no. 2 (Winter 1987).

"Momentum Is Always the Weapon." *Neon* (Nevada State Council on the Arts) (Fall/Winter 1986).

"Warfare." *Cream City Review* 10, no. 2 (1986).

"Be Careful What You Want." *Paris Review* (Fall 1985).

"Revenge." *Northern Lights* (August 1985).

"Freedom." *Black Warrior Review* (Fall 1984).

"Agriculture." *Slackwater Review* (Fall 1984).

"Agriculture." PEN/NEA Syndication Award. *San Francisco Chronicle* (July 22, 1984).

"The Waterfowl Tree." *Syracuse Scholar* (May 1984).

"Blue Stone." *Ploughshares* (Spring 1984).

"Stoneboat." *Montana Eagle* (April 1981).

"No More Money." *Western Star* (December 1980).

"Performing Arts." *TriQuarterly* (Spring 1980).

Excerpt from "Sixty Million Buffalo." *Rocky Mountain Magazine* (December 1979).

"We Are Not in This Together." *TriQuarterly* (Fall 1979).

"Momentum Is Always the Weapon." *Portland Review* 25 (1979).

"One More Time." *Portland Review* 25 (1979).

"Breaking of Glass." *Scratchgravel Hills* (1979).

"Good Boys." *Slackwater Review* (1979).

"Phantom Silver." *Iowa Review* 8, no. 4 (1977).

"Stoneboat." *Oregon East* (1977).

"The Mercy of the Elements." *TriQuarterly* (Spring 1976).

"Kookooskia." *Chariton Review* 1, no. 2 (1975).

"The Vineland Lullaby." *Ploughshares* 2, no. 3 (1975).

"Medusa." *Spectrum* (1975).

"The Stone Corral." *TriQuarterly* (Winter 1974).

"The Man Who Loved Buzzards." *Carolina Quarterly* (1974).

"Unnecessary Beasts." *Sequoia* (1974).

"The Vineland Lullaby." *Tales* (1974).

"Breaker of Horses." *Antioch Review* 32, no. 4 (1973).

"Horses in Heaven." *Ark River Review* (1973).

"Blue Stone." *Ohio Journal* (1973).

"Sometimes There's Nothing There." *Falcon* (Winter 1972).

"Sunday Love." *Fiction* 1, no. 3 (1972).

"The Van Gogh Field." *Iowa Review* (1972).

"Silver and Gold." *North American Review* (1972).

"Thirty-Four Seasons of Winter." *Quarry* (1972).

"Agriculture." *TransPacific* (1972).

"The Underground River." *Atlantic* (1971).

"Autumn on Steens Mountain." *Bullfrog Information Service* (1971).

"Images of Spiritual Childhood." *Sumac* (1971).

"The Red Room." *December* 12 (1970).

"Center of Winter." *Iowa State Liquor Store* (Winter 1970).

"Native Cutthroat." *Northwest Review* (1970).

"The Cove." *Descant* (1968).

"The Voice of Water." *Minnesota Review* (1967).

"The Waterfowl Tree." *Northwest Review* (1966–67).

"Society of Eros." *Northwest Review* (1965–66).

ESSAYS

"The Western Front." *New York Times Magazine* (May 2, 1999).

"Hole in the Sky." *Travel and Leisure Golf* (May/June 1999).

"Tucson: A Way to Love the World." *Travel and Leisure Golf* (September/October 1998).

"The Golden Hotel." *Sunset* (September 1998).

"Otey Island." *Open Spaces* (Spring 1998).

"Doing Good Work Together." *On the Wild Side: Journal of American Wildlands* (Winter 1998).

"Farming in the Free World." *Big Sky Journal* (Spring 1997).

"The Wild West's Not So Natural Disasters." *New York Times* (January 10, 1997).

"We Montanans." *Montana Magazine* (November/December 1996).

"Profile: Jon A. Jackson." *Big Sky Journal* (Summer 1996).

"Golf in Some Best Places." *Big Sky Journal* (Summer 1995).

"He Said/She Said." *Modern Maturity* (May/June 1996).

"The War for Montana's Soul." *Newsweek* (April 15, 1996).

"Profile: Ivan Doig." *Big Sky Journal* (Spring 1996).

Excerpt from *Hole in the Sky. Desert Ramblings: Newsletter of the Oregon High Desert Association* (Spring 1996).

"Innocence." *Iowa Review* 25, no. 2 (Fall 1995).

"Cave." *Wild Duck Review* (June/July 1995).

"The Bluest Water, or Getting to the Bottom of Things." *Missoula Independent* (June 21, 1995).

"Introduction: Cowboy Nation." *Outside* (April 1995).

"Moon." *Talking River Review* (Spring 1995).

"Profile: Ralph Beer." *Big Sky Journal* (Winter 1995).

From *Hole in the Sky. Double Dealer Redux* (Fall 1994).

"Bloom Towns." *Rocky Mountain Magazine* (Summer 1994).

"Second Chance at Paradise." *Audubon* (June 1994).

"Foreword." *Best of Writers at Work* (June 1994).

"Where Our Dreams Chose to Live." *Big Sky Journal* (Spring 1994).

"In the New West." *German GEO* (March 1994).

"Yellowstone in Winter." *Yellowstone Journal* (Winter 1994).

"Robert Helm." Helm Exhibit, Blaffer Gallery Catalogue, University of Houston Press, 1994.

"Home Landscape." *Landscape in America.* Edited by George Thompson. Austin: University of Texas Press, 1994.

"All the Pretty Highways." *Outside* (August 1993).

"Death of the Western." *Culturefront: A Magazine of the Humanities* (New York Council for the Humanities) (Summer 1993).

"Montana: The Last Literary Frontier." *Image Magazine, San Francisco Sunday Examiner* (December 6, 1992).

"Lost Cowboys (But Not Forgotten)." *Antaeus* (Fall 1992).

"Every Thing, Any Where, All of Us." *Manoa* (Fall 1992).

"Montana." *Departures* (August/September 1992).

"Deep Plowing in the Pastures of Heaven." *Neon* (Summer 1992).

"Doing Good Work Together." *Northern Lights* (Summer 1992).

Excerpt from *Owning It All. Wild Oregon* (Summer 1992).

"Falling." *Modern Maturity* (April/May 1992).

"The Best That Can Be: The Politics of Storytelling." *Halcyon* (Spring 1992).

"Ambition." *Hayden's Ferry Review* (Spring 1992).

"Trickery." *Ploughshares* (Spring 1992).

"Walking in Water." *Countryside* (March 1992).

"Desire and Pursuit of the Whole." *Montana: The Magazine of Western History* (Winter 1992).

"White People in Paradise." *Esquire* (December 1991).

"A Saving Light." *Outside* (September 1991).

"Leaving the Ranch." *CutBank* (Spring 1991).

"Perfect Light." *British Vogue* (January 1991).

"Bulletproof." *Ploughshares* (Winter 1990–91).

"Clockwork Agriculture." *Ranching* (Abbeyville Press) (Fall 1989).

"Vanishing." *Kinesis* (Summer 1989).

"Oasis." *Condé Nast Traveler* (March 1989).

"Peaks and Valleys." *Travel and Leisure* (March 1989).

"Ghosts." *Witness* (Winter 1989).

"Gifts." *Northwest Magazine* (December 1988).

"In My Backyard: The Nuclear Dump." *Harper's* (October 1988).

"Montana Renaissance."*Last Best Place* (Fall 1988).

"Searching for the Dutchman: Profile of Bob Corbin." *Pursuits* (Fall 1988).

"Louis L'Amour's West: Myth Was Just a Lie." *Los Angeles Times* (June 23, 1988).

"Robert Redford." *American Health* (April 1988).

"Who Won the West?" *Harper's* (April 1988).

"The Turkey Herders." University of Montana Foundation (December 1987).

"Redneck Secrets." *Harper's* (October 1987).

"Overthrust Dreams." *Outside* (October 1987).

"Owning It All." *Landmark: A Journal of One Thousand Friends of Oregon* (Fall 1987).

"Empire by the Sea." *Outside* (September 1987).

"Montana Rollout." *Outside* (June 1987).

"Owning It All." *Halcyon* (1987).

With Steven M. Krauzer. "Mr. Montana Revisited: Another Look at Granville Stewart." *Montana: The Magazine of Western History* (Autumn 1986).

"Doors to Our House." *Northern Lights* (January/ February 1986).

"New to the Country." *Montana: Magazine of Western History* (Winter 1986).

"Country and Western Stories." *Cream City Review* 10, no. 2 (1986).

With Steven M. Krauzer. "Marshall Joe LeFors versus Killer Tom Horn." *American West* (November/ December 1985).

Miscellaneous excerpts. *National Wildlife Treasury* (November 1985).

"All of Our Friends." *Northern Lights* (January 1985).

"Yellowstone in Winter." *Dial* (November 1984).

With Annick Smith. "The Two Worlds of Norman Maclean: Interviews in Montana and Chicago." *TriQuarterly* (Summer 1984).

"Initiation of a Buckaroo." *Northwest Orient Magazine* (May 1984).

"Xenophobia: Montana Style." *Washington Post* (April 1984).

"Seeing the Elephant: Arts in the Rockies." U.S. Information Agency (1984).

"Owning It All." *Pacific Northwest Magazine* (October 1983).

"Natural Causes." *American West* (September 1983).

"Silver Bullets." *The Movies* (June 1983).

"High Roads." *Outside* (June 1983).

"New Country." *X-C Skier* (November 1982).

"Dialogue with Richard Hugo." *Northwest Review* (Fall 1982).

"Grizzly Too Close." *Outside* (December 1981/January 1982).

"Overthrust Dreams." *Outside* (June 1981).

"The Size of Things." *Pacific Northwest Magazine* (June 1981).

"Drinking with Students." *Rolling Stone* (April 1981).

"Owyhee Buckaroo." *Rocky Mountain Magazine* (September 1980).

With Steven M. Krauzer. "Writers of the New West." *TriQuarterly* (Spring 1980).

"The Family Ranch." *Rocky Mountain Magazine* (January 1980).

"Montana of the Mind." *Outside* (October/November 1979).

"Redneck Secrets." *Rocky Mountain Magazine* (March 1979).

With Steven M. Krauzer. "The Great American Detective." *Armchair Detective* (1978).

"Under Shasta." *Northwest Review* 13, no. 2 (1973).

"The Snow Never Falls Forever." *Harper's* (November 1972).

BOOK INTRODUCTIONS

"West of Your Town: Another Country." Introduction to *The Portable Western Reader,* edited by William Kittredge. New York: Penguin, 1997.

"How to Love This World." Introduction to *Big Sky Country: A View of Paradise: The Best of Montana, North Dakota, Wyoming, and Idaho*. Photographs by Michael Melford. New York: Rizzoli International Publications, 1996.

"Notions of Desire." Foreword to *Just Past Labor Day*, by Kirk Robertson. Reno: University of Nevada Press, 1996.

Introduction to *Yamsi: A Year in the Life of a Wilderness Ranch*, by Dayton O. Hyde. 1971. Reprint, Corvallis: Oregon State University Press, 1996.

"Running Horses." Foreword to *Cowboys and Images: The Watercolors of William Matthews*. San Francisco: Chronicle Books, 1994.

"The Way We Used to Be: Montana in the 1930s." Foreword to *The WPA Guide to Montana*. 1939. Reprint, Tucson: University of Arizona Press, 1994.

Introduction to *Murders At Moon Dance,* by A. B. Guthrie Jr. Lincoln: University of Nebraska Press, 1992.

Introduction to *Surveying the Canadian Pacific: Memoir of a Railroad Pioneer,* by R. M. Rylatt. Salt Lake City: University of Utah Press, 1991.

Introduction to *Montana Spaces,* edited by William Kittredge. New York: Nick Lyons Books, 1988.

With Steven M. Krauzer. Introduction to *Fiction to Fiction,* edited by William Kittredge and Steven M. Krauzer. New York: Harper & Row, 1979.

With Steven M. Krauzer. "The Great American Detective." Introduction to *The Great American Detective,* edited by William Kittredge and Steven M. Krauzer. New York: New American Library, 1978.

With Steven M. Krauzer. Introduction to *Great Action Stories,* edited by William Kittredge and Steven M. Krauzer. New York: New American Library, 1977.

ANTHOLOGY APPEARANCES

Excerpt from "Owning It All." In *The Graywolf Silver Anthology,* edited by Fiona McCrae. St. Paul: Graywolf Press, 1999.

"Reimagining Warner." In *The Literary West,* edited by Thomas J. Lyon. New York: Oxford University Press, 1999.

"Second Chance at Paradise." In *Literature and the Environment: A Reader on Nature and Culture,* edited by Lorraine Anderson, Scott Slovic, and John P. O'Grady. New York: Addison Wesley Longman, 1999.

"Thirty-Four Seasons of Winter." In *The Workshop: Seven Decades of Fiction from the Iowa Writers' Workshop,* edited by Tom Grimes. New York: Hyperion, 1999.

"Where Our Dreams Choose to Live." In *The Big Sky Reader,* edited by Allen Jones and Jeff Wetmore. New York: St. Martin's Press, 1998.

"Trickery." In *Of Frogs and Toads,* edited by Jill Carpenter. Sewanee, Tenn.: Ione Press, 1998.

"Who Owns the West?" In *Readings in American Indian Law,* edited by Jo Carrillo. Philadelphia: Temple University Press, 1998.

"Inside the Earth." In *Reclaiming the Native Home of Hope,* edited by Robert Keiter. Salt Lake City: University of Utah Press, 1998.

"Where Our Dreams Choose to Live." In *The Best of Big Sky Journal,* vol. 1, edited by Allen Jones and

Jeff Wetmore. Bozeman, Mont.: Spring Creek Publishing, 1997.

"Overthrust Dreams." In *The Best of Outside: The First Twenty Years,* edited by the editors of *Outside.* New York: Villard, 1997.

"Images of Spiritual Parenthood." In *The Sumac Reader,* edited by Joseph Bednarik. East Lansing, Mich.: Michigan State University Press, 1997.

"Eating Ourselves Alive." In *Waste Land: Meditations on a Ravaged Landscape.* Photographs by David T. Hanson. New York: Aperture, 1997.

"Taking Our Turn, or Responsibilities." In *The Geography of Hope: A Tribute to Wallace Stegner,* edited by Mary Stegner and Page Stegner. San Francisco: Sierra Club Books, 1996.

"Poisoning the Rivers." In *Headwaters: Montana Writers on Water and Wilderness,* edited by Annick Smith. Missoula, Mont.: Hellgate Writers, 1996.

"Interlude." In *In Short: A Collection of Brief Creative Nonfiction,* edited by Judith Kitchen and Mary Paumier Jones. New York: Norton, 1996.

"Timothy O'Sullivan." In *Perpetual Mirage: Photographic Narratives of the Desert West,* edited by May Castleberry. New York: Whitney Museum, 1996.

"Taking Care of Our Horses." In *The Place Within: Portaits of the American Landscape by Contemporary Writers,* edited by Jodi Daynard. New York: Norton, 1996.

"The Bluest Water, or Getting to the Bottom of Things." In *The Sacred Place: Witnessing the Holy in the Physical World,* edited by W. Scott Olsen and Scott Cairns. Salt Lake City: University of Utah Press, 1996.

"Sanity." In *Testimony: Writers of the West Speak On Behalf of Utah Wilderness,* compiled by Stephen Trimble and Terry Tempest Williams. Minneapolis: Milkweed Editions, 1996.

"The Good Rain: Stegner and the Wild." In *Wallace Stegner: Man and Writer,* edited by Charles E. Rankin. Albuquerque: University of New Mexico Press, 1996.

"We Are Not in This Together." In *Fiction 100: An Anthology of Short Stories,* edited by James H. Pickering. New Jersey: Prentice Hall, 1995.

"Do You Hear Your Mother Talking?" In *From the Island's Edge: A Sitka Reader,* edited by Carolyn Servid. St. Paul: Graywolf Press, 1995.

"Who Owns the West?" In *Modern American Memoirs,* edited by Annie Dillard and Cort Conley. New York: Harper Collins, 1995.

"Sanity." In *Testimony: Writers of the West Speak On Behalf of Utah Wilderness,* compiled by Stephen Trimble and Terry Tempest Williams. Printed in Salt Lake City for distribution to the U.S. Congress, 1995.

"Home." In *Best American Essays for College Students,* edited by Robert Atwan. Boston: Houghton Mifflin, 1994.

"Lost Cowboys (But Not Forgotten)." In *Best Nature Writing, 1994,* edited by John A. Murray. San Francisco: Sierra Club Books, 1994.

"Reimagining Warner." In *Heart of the Land: Essays on the Last Great Places,* edited by Joseph Barbato and Lisa Weinerman. New York: Pantheon, 1994.

"Looking Glass." In *Listening to Ourselves,* edited by Alan Cheuse and Caroline Marshall. New York: Doubleday, 1994.

Excerpt from "Owning It All." In *Being in the World: An Environmental Reader for Writers,* edited by Scott H. Slovic and Terrell F. Dixon. New York: Macmillan, 1993.

"Do You Hear Your Mother Talking." In *Dreamers and Desperadoes,* edited by Craig Lesley. New York: Dell, 1993.

"Doing Good Work Together." In *The True Subject: Writers on Life and Craft,* edited by Kurt Brown. St. Paul: Graywolf Press, 1993.

"Who Won the West?" In *Turning Toward Home: Reflections on the Family from Harper's Magazine,* edited by Katharine Wittemore. New York: Harper's Magazine Foundation, 1993.

"Native Cutthroat." In *The World Begins Here: An Anthology of Oregon Short Fiction,* edited by Glen A. Love. Corvallis: Oregon State University Press, 1993.

Excerpt from "Owning It All." In *Cultural Tapestry: Readings for a Pluralistic Society,* edited by Faun Evans, Barbara Gleason, and Mark Wiley. New York: Addison Wesley, 1992.

"Three Dollar Dogs." In *Fathers and Sons,* edited by David Seybold. New York: Grove, 1992.

"Grizzly: 1987." In *The Great Bear,* edited by John A. Murray. Seattle: Alaska Northwest Books, 1992.

"New to the Country." In *Montana Heritage,* edited by Robert W. Swarthout Jr. and Harry Fritz. Helena, Mont.: Montana Historical Society Press, 1992.

"Home." In *New Writers of the Purple Sage,* edited by Russell Martin. New York: Penguin, 1992.

"Ghosts." In *On Nature's Terms,* edited by Thomas J. Lyon and Peter Stine. College Station: Texas A&M University Press, 1992.

"Overthrust Dreams." In *Out of the Noosphere: The Best of Outside Magazine,* edited by Mark Bryant. New York: Simon & Schuster, 1992.

"Yellowstone in Winter." In *Wilderness Tapestry,* edited by Mikel Vause, William McVaugh, and Samuel Zeveloff. Reno: University of Nevada Press, 1992.

"Agriculture." In *A Society to Match the Scenery,* edited by Gary Holthaus. Boulder: University of Colorado Press, 1991.

"Who Owns the West?" In *Best American Essays: 1989,* edited by Geoffrey Wolff. New York: Ticknor & Fields, 1989.

"Redneck Secrets." In *The Pushcart Prize Thirteen,* edited by Bill Henderson. New York: Viking Penguin, 1989.

"Home." In *Best American Essays: 1988,* edited by Annie Dillard. New York: Ticknor & Fields, 1988.

"The Underground River." In *The Best of the West,* edited by James Thomas. Salt Lake City: Peregrine Smith Books, 1988.

"Owyhee Buckaroo." In *East of Eden—West of Zion,* edited by Wilbur S. Shepperson. Reno: University of Nevada Press, 1988.

"Phantom Silver." In *Graywolf Annual Four: Short Stories by Men,* edited by Scott Walker. St. Paul: Graywolf Press, 1988.

"Drinking and Driving." In *Graywolf Annual Three: Essays, Memoirs and Reflections,* edited by Scott Walker. St. Paul: Graywolf Press, 1987.

"New to the Country." In *Northwest Variety,* edited by Lex Runciman. Corvallis, Oreg.: Arrowood Books, 1987.

"Dialogue with Richard Hugo." In *The Real West Marginal Way: A Poet's Autobiography,* edited by

Ripley S. Hugo, James Welch, and Lois M. Welch.
New York: Norton, 1986.

"Agriculture." In *The Pushcart Prize Ten: Best of the Small Presses*, edited by Bill Henderson. Wainscott, Conn.: Pushcart Press, 1985–86.

"Stoneboat." In *The Available Press/PEN Short Story Collection*, edited by Anne Tyler. New York: Ballantine Books, 1985.

"We Are Not in This Together." In *Writers of the Purple Sage*, edited by Russell Martin and Marc Barasch. New York: Viking/Penguin, 1984.

"Thirty-Four Seasons of Winter." In *Matters of Life and Death: New American Stories*, edited by Tobias Wolff. New York: Wampeta Press, 1982.

"The Van Gogh Field." In *Fiction of the Far West*, edited by James D. Houston. New York: Bantam Books, 1980.

"The Waterfowl Tree." In *Stories That Count*, edited by William Roecker. New York: Holt, Rinehart and Winston, 1971.

FILM CREDITS

A River Runs Through It. Coassociate producer. Wildwood Productions, 1992.

With Norman Maclean. Screenplay adaptation. *A River Runs Through It.* Star Route Productions, 1986.

Windbreak. Screenplay. New Front Films, 1988.

Peacock's War. Associate producer. National Public Television, 1988.

Heartland. Script consultant and writer. Wilderness Women, Inc., 1979.

SOUND RECORDINGS

Interviewed by Michael Silverblatt. *Bookworm.*
KCRW-Public Radio, Los Angeles, California,
1996.

"Interview with William Kittredge." Interviewed by
Rebecca Newth. KUAF, Fayetteville, Arkansas,
1993.

"Looking Glass." National Public Radio, 1993.

"The West of Wallace Stegner." Canadian Public
Radio, 1993.

"Montana Writers." National Public Radio, November
1989.

"Three Dollar Dogs." National Public Radio, Fall 1989.

Interview. *Morning Edition,* National Public Radio,
September 1992.

Interview. *Fresh Air,* National Public Radio, August
1992.

"Drinking and Driving." *Listener's Bookstall,* KUFM,
1988.

"Owning It All." National Public Radio, September 11,
1987.

Interview. *Fresh Air,* National Public Radio, 1987.

VIDEO RECORDINGS

Interview. "Art of the Wild." Foundation for Global
Community, 1996. (222 High Street, Palo Alto, CA
94301; 415-328-7756.)

Good Morning America. ABC, November 1995.

"Great Drives of America" (Highway 93). PBS, 1995.

"West Words." Produced by Jean Walkinshaw. PBS
documentary, 1995.

Interview. Montana Committee for the Humanities, September 1993.
Today Show. NBC, July 4, 1989.

INTERVIEWS

Anonymous. "William Kittredge: At Home off the Range." On Campus: *Official Publication of the American Federation of Teachers* (May/June 1994).

Blewitt, Peter. "Interview with William Kittredge." *Cream City Review* 10, no. 2 (1986).

Gonzalez, Ray. "Myth of Ownership: An Interview with Bill Kittredge." *Bloomsbury Review* 8, no. 4 (July/August 1988).

Long, David. "Interview with William Kittredge." *Poets & Writers* 15, no. 2 (March/April 1987).

Morris, Greg. "William Kittredge." *Talking Up a Storm: Voices of the New West.* Lincoln: University of Nebraska Press, 1994.

Nelson, Barbara, and Wendy White-Ring. "Interview with William Kittredge." *Hayden's Ferry Review* (Spring/Summer 1991).

Newth, Rebecca. "Interview with William Kittredge." *Arkansas Democrat and Gazette* (November 26, 1993).

Walker, Casey. "An Interview: William Kittredge and Annick Smith." *Wild Duck Review* (June/July 1995).

Ward, Amanda. "Interview with William Kittredge." *CutBank* 48 (Fall 1997).

Webb, Benjamin. "Writers and Geographers." *Fugitive Faith: Conversations on Spiritual, Environmental and Community Renewal.* Maryknoll, N.Y.: Orbis Books, 1998.

BIOGRAPHICAL/CRITICAL STUDIES AND BOOK REVIEWS

Arthur, Anthony. "The Van Gogh Field and Other Stories." *Western American Literature* (Fall 1979).

Baker, Will. "Cord: A Sidesaddle Soap with a Rawhide Twist." *Missoulian* (May 15, 1982).

Blaise, Brian. Review of *The Portable Western Reader. Big Sky Journal* (Fall 1997).

Blew, Mary Clearman. "William Kittredge." *Updating the Literary West,* edited by Thomas J. Lyon. Fort Worth: Texas Christian University Press, 1997.

Brazil, Eric. Review of *Hole in the Sky. Sunday San Francisco Examiner and Chronicle* (June 28, 1992).

Buchholtz, C. W. "Dose of Reality. . . ." *Rocky Mountain News* (March 10, 1996).

Carlin, Margaret. "No Longer at Home on the Range." *Rocky Mountain News* (July 19, 1992).

Carver, Raymond. "Bluebird Mornings, Storm Warnings." *San Francisco Review of Books* (July 1979). Reprinted in *American Book Review* (October 1979).

———. "Van Gogh Field: Troubling and Unforgettable Stories of the West." *Tempo* (August 25, 1979).

Cassell, Faris. "Reworking the Myths of the West." *Eugene Register-Guard* (March 3, 1996).

Chatham, Russell. Review of *We Are Not in This Together. Outside* (November 1979).

Conner, K. Patrick. "Failing the Land, Failing the Soul." *San Francisco Chronicle* (August 2, 1992).

Crumley, James. "Van Gogh Field, Other Stories." *Rocky Mountain Magazine* (June 1979).

Desowitz, Bill. Review of *Stories into Film. Film Quarterly* (Summer 1981).

Dold, Gerald. "Haunting Tale Achingly Told." *Wichita Eagle* (August 30, 1992).

"Don't Fence Them Out." *Newsweek* (July 13, 1992).

Drabelle, Dennis. "In Praise of the Great Outdoors." *Washington Post Book World* (April 14, 1996). Reprinted in *Tampa Tribune and Times* (April 21, 1996).

Duane, Daniel. "How the West Might Someday Be Won." *Los Angeles Times Book Review* (February 11, 1996).

Dykhuis, Randy. Review of *Owning It All. Library Journal* (August 1987).

———. Review of *Who Owns the West? Library Journal* (December 1995).

Elrod, Rof. Review of *We Are Not in This Together. St. Petersburg Times* (July 29, 1984).

Fleming, Walter C. Review of *The Last Best Place. American Indian Quarterly* (Fall 1990).

Fotheringham, Chris. Review of *Who Owns the West? Santa Barbara News-Press* (February 25, 1996).

Glover, Charlotte L. Review of *The Portable Western Reader. Library Journal* (July 1997).

Grover, Jan Zita. "The Emblematic Grizzly." *Hungry Mind Review* (Summer 1996).

Gurley, George. "Stories Are a Form of Poetic Journalism." *Kansas City Star* (December 17, 1978).

Harding, William Harry. Review of *We Are Not in This Together. Westways* (October 1984).

Harvey, Miles. Review of *Who Owns the West? Outside* (March 1996).

Hays, Dan. Review of *Who Owns the West? Salem Statesman-Journal* (March 3, 1996).

Helig, Steve. "This Land Is Our Land." *San Francisco Examiner and Chronicle Book World* (March 10, 1996).

Heltzel, Ellen Emry. "Lamentation on the Land." *Sunday Oregonian* (February 25, 1996).

Hepworth, James. Review of *Hole in the Sky*. *Bloomsbury Review* (July/August 1992).

Hooper, Brad. Review of *The Portable Western Reader*. *Booklist* (June 1, 1997).

Hugo, Richard. "Heroes of the West." *Portland Review* 25 (1979).

Johnson, Jerry. "Two Writers in Search of America." *Deseret News* (June 7, 1992).

Juillerat, Lee. Review of *Hole in the Sky*. *Klamath Falls Herald and News* (July 19, 1992).

Knickerbocker, Brad. Review of *Hole in the Sky*. *Christian Science Monitor* (July 23, 1992).

Kosak, Stephen. "Little Magazines: A Quarterly Report." *Chicago Tribune* (August 24, 1980).

Leach, Sharon J. "Reimagining the West." *Terrain* (June 1996).

Lehmann-Haupt, Christopher. Review of *Hole in the Sky*. *New York Times* (June 8, 1992).

Love, Glen A. "Place and Confidence." *Northwest Review* 26, no. 2 (1988).

Maguire, James H. Review of *The Last Best Place*. *Journal of the West* (October 1990).

Marshall, John. "Westward Hope." *Seattle Post-Intelligencer* (March 9, 1996). Reprinted as "How the West Went Wrong." *Kansas City Star* (March 31, 1998).

Martin, Russell. "William Kittredge's World-Weary West." *Pacific Northwest Magazine* (June 1984).

McCabe, Carol. "Gone West." *Providence Journal* (July 19, 1992).

Merriam, Ginny. Review of *Hole in the Sky. Missoulian* (May 31, 1992).

Merrill, Christopher. Review of *Hole in the Sky. Orion* (Winter 1994).

———. Review of *Owning It All. New England Review and Bread Loaf Quarterly* (Winter 1989).

Miller, Kevin. "Shooting Down the Gunslinger." *Eugene Register-Guard* (August 2, 1992).

Morris, Gregory. Review of *Hole in the Sky. Magill Book Reviews* (Dow Jones On-Line News Retrieval) (1993).

———. "The Rocky Mountains." *Updating the Literary West.* Edited by Thomas J. Lyon. Fort Worth: Texas Christian University Press, 1997.

Murray, John A. Review of *Who Owns the West? Bloomsbury Review* (July/August 1996).

Mutter, John. Review of *Owning It All. Publishers Weekly* (May 22, 1987).

Nicholas, Jonathan. "How the West Was Won." *Oregonian* (December 1, 1992).

"New in Paperback." *Washington Post Book World* (June 27, 1993).

"Noted with Pleasure." *New York Times Book Review* (July 5, 1992).

Ott, Bill. Review of *Who Owns the West? Booklist* (February 15, 1996).

"Paperbacks." *Arizona Republic* (June 27, 1993).

Penner, Jonathan. "Blue Sky, Red Blood." *New York Times Book Review* (September 9, 1984).

Perrin, Noel. Review of *Hole in the Sky. Washington Post Book World* (May 31, 1992).

Peterson, Andrew. Review of *The Portable Western Reader. Missoulian* (August 10, 1997).

Peterson, Clarence. "The Great American Detective." *Chicago Tribune Book World* (October 28, 1978).

Pintarich, Paul. "Living Through Literature." *Sunday Oregonian* (June 21, 1992).

———. Review of *We Are Not in This Together. Portland Oregonian* (July 29, 1984).

Rees, Tony. Review of *Hole in the Sky. Forewords: The Western Digest of Literary Opinion* (Summer 1992).

Reid, Robert Sims. "Cord Fans Can Settle Back for No. Two." *Missoulian* (September 25, 1982).

Review of *Hole in the Sky. Kirkus Reviews* (May 1, 1992).

Review of *Hole in the Sky. Publishers Weekly* (May 11, 1992).

Review of *The Last Best Place. American West* (June 1989).

Review of *We Are Not in This Together. Kirkus Reviews* (April 15, 1984).

Review of *We Are Not in This Together. Publishers Weekly* (March 30, 1984).

Review of *Who Owns the West? Books of the Southwest* (February 1996).

Review of *Who Owns the West? Bookwatch* (March 1996).

Review of *Who Owns the West? Kirkus Reviews* (November 15, 1995).

Review of *Who Owns the West? Library Journal* (December 6, 1995).

Review of *Who Owns the West? Ogden Standard Examiner* (February 25, 1996).

Review of *Who Owns the West? Publishers Weekly* (December 18, 1995).

Review of *Who Owns the West? Spokane Spokesman-Review* (January 21, 1996).

Robinson, Leonard Wallace. "Kittredge Weaves a Masterpiece." *Missoulian* (March 28, 1985).

Robinson, Lucia St. Clair. "Cord Series Better than the Average Western Fare." *Missoulian* (December 20, 1985).

Rollins, Judy B. "William Kittredge Writes the West." *Salt Lake Tribune* (July 3, 1992).

Sarver, Stephanie. Review of *Who Owns the West? Interdisciplinary Studies in Literature and Environment* 5, no. 1 (Winter 1998).

Schulian, John. "Regrets Like Rain." *Los Angeles Times Book Review* (July 5, 1992). Reprinted as "Western Wreckage." *Outdoor Journal of Salt Lake City* (August/September 1992).

Shattuck, Kathryn. Review of *Who Owns the West? New York Times Book Review* (April 21, 1996).

Simon, Julie Clark. Review of *The Last Best Place. Western Historical Quarterly* (May 1990).

Smiley, Jane. "An American Family in the Landscape." *Chicago Tribune* (July 12, 1992).

Snow, Donald. Review of *Montana Spaces. Sierra* (July/August 1989).

Solomon, Charles. "Paperbacks." *Los Angeles Times Book Review* (July 11, 1993). Reprinted in *Everett Herald* (September 17, 1993).

Steffans, Ron. Review of *The Portable Western Reader. Bloomsbury Review* (September/October 1997).

Steinberg, Sybil. Review of *The Last Best Place. Publishers Weekly* (January 20, 1989).

Testo, Matt. "A New West Is Looking for Some Fresh Myths." *Jackson Hole News* (April 24, 1996).

Wanner, Irene. Review of *Who Owns the West? Seattle Times* (June 30, 1996).

Washburn, Keith. "The Van Gogh Field and Other Stories." *Library Journal* (January 1, 1979).

Wiley, Peter Booth. "How the West Was Undone." *San Francisco Review of Books* (Winter 1992).

Wilson, Robert. Review of *Hole in the Sky. USA Today* (June 19, 1992).

Whittamore, Katherine. Review of *Who Owns the West? Sneakpeeks* (http://www.salonmag.com/06/).

Wolff, Kurt. "Sage Advice." *San Francisco Bay Guardian* (April 24, 1996).

Wortham, Thomas. Review of *The Last Best Place. Nineteenth-Century Literature* (December 1989).

Wulbert, Roland. Review of *Hole in the Sky. Booklist* (June 15, 1992).

Zindel, Tim. Review of *Hole in the Sky. Library Journal* (August 1992).

Zoretich, Frank. Review of *Who Owns the West? Albuquerque Journal* (December 2, 1996).

WORKS CITED

p. 5　　William Kittredge, *Hole in the Sky* (New York: Knopf, 1992).

p. 6　　William Kittredge, *Owning It All* (St. Paul: Graywolf, 1987).

p. 7　　William Kittredge, *Who Owns the West?* (San Francisco: Mercury House, 1996).

p. 14　　Simone Weil, "The *Iliad,* Poem of Might," in *The Simone Weil Reader,* ed. George A. Panichas (New York: David McKay, 1997), 153–83.

p. 16　　Ralph Waldo Emerson, "Self-Reliance," in *The Writings of Ralph Waldo Emerson,* ed. Brook Atkinson (New York: Modern Library, 1950), 148.

p. 23　　Ernest Hemingway, *The Sun Also Rises* (New York: Scribner, 1996), 222.

p. 53　　Aristotle, *The Poetics* (New York: W. W. Norton, 1982).

p. 56   Henry David Thoreau, "Walking," in
             The Natural History Essays (Salt Lake City:
             Peregrine Smith, 1980), 93–136.

p. 67   E. O. Wilson, *Biophilia* (Cambridge, Mass.:
             Harvard University Press, 1984), 121.

p. 71   I. S. Shklovskii and Carl Sagan, *Intelligent
             Life in the Universe,* trans. Paula Fern (San
             Francisco: Holden-Day, 1966).

p. 79   Spinoza, *Ethics* (Indianapolis: Hackett,
             1992).

p. 82   Morris Berman, *The Reenchantment of the
             World* (Ithaca, N.Y.: Cornell University
             Press, 1981).

p. 83   William Kittredge, *Owning It All,* 64.

p. 83   William Kittredge and Steven M. Krauzer,
             "Writers of the New West," *TriQuarterly*
             (Spring 1980): 6.

p. 84   William Kittredge, *Who Owns the West?,*
             147.

pp. 85–86 John Graves, "The Southwest as the
             Cradle of the Writer," lecture presented
             at Southwest Texas State University, San
             Marcos, Texas (October 1978), 11.

pp. 86–87 Kevin Miller, "Shooting Down the
             Gunslinger," an interview with William

Kittredge, *Eugene Register-Guard* (August 2, 1992), H1.

p. 87   William Kittredge, *Hole in the Sky,* 173.

p. 87   William Kittredge, *Owning It All,* 62.

p. 88   William Kittredge, "The Snow Never Falls Forever," *Harper's* (November 1972): 120.

pp. 88–89 William Kittredge, *Owning It All,* 60.

p. 90   William Kittredge, *Owning It All,* 61, 62, 74.

p. 91   William Kittredge, *Hole in the Sky,* 126, 152, 149.

pp. 91–92 William Kittredge, *Hole in the Sky,* 153.

p. 92   William Kittredge, *Hole in the Sky,* 171, 177–178.

p. 93   William Kittredge, *Owning It All,* 74, 75.

p. 93   William Kittredge, *Hole in the Sky,* 217.

p. 94   Glen A. Love, "Place and Confidence," review of *Owning It All, Northwest Review* 26, no. 2 (1988): 135.

p. 95   William Kittredge, *Hole in the Sky,* 31.

p. 96   Jane Smiley, review of *Hole in the Sky, Chicago Tribune* (July 12, 1992), 7.

pp. 96–97 William Kittredge, "Second Chance at Paradise," *Audubon* (June 1994): 35.

p. 97   William Kittredge, "A Saving Light,"
         Outside (September 1991): 73.

p. 99   William Kittredge, "Doing Good Work
         Together," *Who Owns the West?*, 52–53.

SCOTT SLOVIC, founding president of the Association for the Study of Literature and Environment (ASLE), currently serves as editor of the journal *ISLE: Interdisciplinary Studies in Literature and Environment.* He is the author of *Seeking Awareness in American Nature Writing: Henry Thoreau, Annie Dillard, Edward Abbey, Wendell Berry, Barry Lopez* (University of Utah Press, 1992); his coedited books include *Being in the World: An Environmental Reader for Writers* (Macmillan, 1993), *Reading the Earth: New Directions in the Study of Literature and the Environment* (University of Idaho Press, 1998), and *Literature and the Environment: A Reader on Nature and Culture* (Addison Wesley Longman, 1999). Currently he is an associate professor of English and the director of the Center for Environmental Arts and Humanities at the University of Nevada, Reno.

MORE BOOKS ON THE WORLD AS HOME
FROM MILKWEED EDITIONS

To order books or for more information, contact Milkweed at (800) 520-6455 or visit our website (www.milkweed.org).

Brown Dog of the Yaak:
Essays on Art and Activism
Rick Bass

Boundary Waters:
The Grace of the Wild
Paul Gruchow

Grass Roots:
The Universe of Home
Paul Gruchow

The Necessity of Empty Places
Paul Gruchow

A Sense of the Morning:
Field Notes of a Born Observer
David Brendan Hopes

Ecology of a Cracker Childhood
Janisse Ray

The Dream of the Marsh Wren:
Writing As Reciprocal Creation
Pattiann Rogers

The Country of Language
Scott Russell Sanders

The Book of the Tongass
Edited by Carolyn Servid and Donald Snow

Homestead
Annick Smith

Testimony:
Writers of the West Speak
On Behalf of Utah Wilderness
Compiled by Stephen Trimble
and Terry Tempest Williams

OTHER BOOKS OF INTEREST TO
THE WORLD AS HOME READER:

Essays

The Heart Can Be Filled Anywhere on Earth:
Minneota, Minnesota
Bill Holm

Shedding Life:
Disease, Politics, and Other Human Conditions
Miroslav Holub

Children's Novels

No Place
Kay Haugaard

The Monkey Thief
Aileen Kilgore Henderson

Treasure of Panther Peak
Aileen Kilgore Henderson

The Dog with Golden Eyes
Frances Wilbur

Anthologies

Sacred Ground:
Writings about Home
Edited by Barbara Bonner

Verse and Universe:
Poems about Science and Mathematics
Edited by Kurt Brown

Poetry

Boxelder Bug Variations
Bill Holm

THE WORLD AS HOME, the nonfiction publishing program of Milkweed Editions, is dedicated to exploring our relationship to the natural world. Not espousing any particular environmentalist or political agenda, these books are a forum for distinctive literary writing that not only alerts the reader to vital issues but offers personal testimonies to living harmoniously with other species in urban, rural, and wilderness communities.

MILKWEED EDITIONS publishes with the intention of making a humane impact on society, in the belief that literature is a transformative art uniquely able to convey the essential experiences of the human heart and spirit. To that end, Milkweed publishes distinctive voices of literary merit in handsomely designed, visually dynamic books, exploring the ethical, cultural, and esthetic issues that free societies need continually to address. Milkweed Editions is a not-for-profit press.

Typeset in Stone Serif
by Stanton Publication Services, Inc.
Printed on acid-free, recycled
55# Frasier Miami Book Natural paper
by Friesen Corporation